Hair Today, Gone Tomorrow

RANDY FISHELL

Hair Today, Gone Tomorrow

REVIEW AND HERALD® PUBLISHING ASSOCIATION
HAGERSTOWN, MD 21740

The author assumes full responsibility for the accuracy of
all facts and quotations cited in this book.

Unless otherwise noted, all Scripture quotations are from the *Holy Bible, New
International Version*. Copyright © 1973, 1978, 1984, International Bible
Society. Used by permission of Zondervan Bible Publishers.

This book was
Edited by Tim Lale·
Cover design by Bill Kirstein
Cover illustration by Roger Roth
Typeset: Palatino 10.5/12

PRINTED IN U.S.A.

00 99 98 97 96   5 4 3 2 1

R&H Cataloging Service
Fishell, Randy
    Hair today, gone tomorrow.

    1. Christian life. 2. Spiritual life.
3. Religious life. I. Title.

        248.8

ISBN 0-8280-1056-0

DEDICATION

The above quality is something
Mom and Dad needed a lot of,
trying to nurture me
along the path toward maturity.
It's a trait I hope Tyler, Andrew, and Ethan
find abundant in their father's life
as well.

FOREWORD

"Why don't you just grow up?"

Originally spoken by budding horticulturists, this pithy adage has become a favorite of parents caught between desiring the best for their children and the comfort of a padded cell.

Truth is, as we try to become a people of genuine good character, we can *all* stand a little growing. I believe this book contains some seed thoughts that will spur you on toward a more substantive selfhood.

In these foible-filled chapters, I've used my creative license from time to time, something I keep in my wallet for just such occasions. Yet the basic incidents that typically left me in a less-than-enviable position are regrettably true.

As you will probably guess if you stick with this book to the end, I'm hardly a paradigm of virtue. But I *have* managed to grow, if not all the way up. Maybe what I've gleaned can help you in your quest to become a real character, or better still, to develop a pretty good one.

CONTENTS

Truth
Tip #1

Work
on the Inside

HAIR TODAY, GONE TOMORROW

The shock hit me as I looked in the mirror. *Can it really be happening to me? I'm too young!* This curse knows no favorites. I was going bald.

Now, we're not talking about an occasional strand turning up missing. I appeared headed for a dyed-in-the-wool chrome dome. Paranoia began to set in. Little children would snicker at my shiny top as they passed me on the sidewalk. And I could forget romance. Who would want to go out with, let alone marry, a certified melon-head?

I would have to keep this malady under my hat. But how?

I remembered seeing ads in the local newspaper for the scalp-analysis clinic at the Holiday Inn "for two days only." Before-and-after photos showed an overhead shot of a bald-headed man. That was the "before." On the other side of the ad, the same man had sprouted a crop of hair. Maybe it would work for me too.

A new thought struck me. Somehow, going to Room 215 at the Holiday Inn seemed a little like going to an adult bookstore. What if somebody saw me?

I called a friend in Tennessee who's a fellow sufferer.

He said, "Randy, I've discovered the secret to regrowing hair . . . alfalfa pills."

"Is that a fact?" It made sense. Cows thrive on alfalfa; I've never seen a bald guernsey. But what if it took effect *all over* my body? I could see the headline: "Missing Link Found in Southwestern Michigan—Alive!" I needed professional counseling.

As I looked in the White Pages for the number of a dermatologist, I began thinking. *Maybe baldness wouldn't be so bad after all. If I get married, I might have kids someday. That could make me want* to tear my hair out. *No problem for a slickie! But then I might become top billing for those same youngsters' neighborhood circus: "Come see the man with an ostrich egg head!"*

The receptionist scheduled an appointment for two weeks away. I hoped there would still be something left to diagnose.

On the right day, I slunk into the dermatologist's waiting room. I prayed that some gorgeous RN would not come and ask me what I wanted to see the doctor about.

Enter cover-girl nurse.

"Well, uh . . ." I cleared my throat. "I think I'm, well, going bald."

I never did like pretty girls who snort when they laugh.

The doctor brought in a two-by-three-foot picture of a hair shaft that looked like a giant sequoia. He asked me about my family's hair history. I told him Mom had quite a bit, and Dad didn't have *any*. I knew I was in trouble, but the doctor said there might yet be some hope.

"You see, there's just no way of telling how long your hair will continue to fall out. It might even stop tomorrow. You could end up going through life with a full head of hair."

Now that sounded encouraging. This doctor obviously knew what he was talking about.

"On the other hand," he continued, "your hair might keep falling out until there's nothing left at all."

I never did like doctors who snort when they laugh. I left his office wondering if I should stop by the local pool hall and apply for a job as a cue ball.

Right about then I remembered the scientist. He lived just outside of town and had invented some sort of hair-growing medicine. The story went that he'd completed the experimentation, but he still had not raised money to put the stuff into production. It was my last hope. I headed over to the scientist's lab.

A little man came to the door and asked me what I wanted. I told him I'd come for a jar of the "stuff."

"It's not ready until six o'clock tonight," he said, peering through the door opening. "Five dollars for one bottle. You come back at six o'clock."

Not sure what I was getting my head into, I returned at the appointed time. The little man told me to wait outside, and a few moments later he returned with a jar filled with green jelly.

"Now, you rub medicine on bald spots twice a day—yes? Once in the morning, once at night. I rub all over my head—leave on all day. It greasy, but what you want, greasy hair or bald head?"

I never did like scientists who snort when they laugh. But I paid him the money and drove off to begin my therapy.

At home, I ran upstairs and locked the bathroom door behind me. Opening the jar, I dipped my finger in and scooped out a glob of the green goop. I patted it onto the thinning areas of my hair, convinced that before long I would be eternally indebted to the stuff for restoring my virility.

And then the most astonishing thing happened. Not *on* my head, but *in* it. Staring at myself in the mirror, I realized that concern with the way I look had made me forget how people *saw* me. Did Mom and Dad love me just because I happened to have a full head of hair? The first time they saw me I was bald, and they loved me anyway!

And what about that surprise birthday party my friends gave me last month? My molting pate didn't keep them from their good deed. With or without hair, I was worthy in their eyes because of *me*, not a jarful of green jelly.

I tossed the follicle fertilizer aside and went in search of a soft-bristle brush—the kind that feels good on bare skin. My hair-raising experience was over.

Truth Tip #2

Consider the Outcome of Your Choices

"SURELY I HAVE ACTED LIKE A FOOL AND HAVE ERRED GREATLY"
(1 SAMUEL 26:21).

HOT STUFF

Everybody makes a bad choice from time to time. Small-time crooks seem to have a special knack for making bad choices, above and beyond their original crimes.

Take Tony M., of Pittsburgh, Pennsylvania. Tony broke into a city building and discovered a Polaroid camera in one of the offices. He decided to take a picture of himself. When it came out black, he tossed it into a trash can.

Bad choice.

"He didn't understand how the camera works," a police officer commented. "It takes a little time for the film to develop."

Armed with a copy of the photo, a police officer spotted Tony strolling in downtown Pittsburgh, looking the very picture of innocence. He was snapped again—this time holding a prison ID number at chest level.

Then there was the bank robber in Detroit, Michigan, who ran down the street from a couple of armed guards. The crook dodged into what he thought was an apartment building.

Bad choice. It was the police station.*

Let's turn to the Michigan Fire Maniacs. This fun-loving group of five young teens boasted a collective IQ that matched the local fire department's opinion of them—very low. I write with some authority on this topic as a former card-carrying member of this wacky outfit.

The Brawley brothers had invited several of us guys over to their grandparents' farm for Sabbath lunch. After we'd inhaled the last of Grandma Brawley's fine apple pie, the five of us politely excused ourselves and set off in search of some fine Sabbath afternoon mischief.

Quickly Spike Brawley and Buddy Mitchell steered us in the right—er, wrong—direction. Over the driveway and through the field to Grandmother's woods we went.

Understand that summer Michigan woods approach the fire potential of a Kuwaiti oil field in a drought. That's why I questioned the wisdom of Spike's pulling a few firecrackers and a book of matches from his pocket. *Something tells me this is a* very *bad choice,* I thought.

"These babies came from Tennessee," Spike informed us. "Got 'em on the way back from our vacation in Florida." We watched with some admiration as Spike struck a match and put it to the fuse. A split second later a loud *bang!* shot through the woods.

"Hey, Spike, you'd better cool it," his usually quiet brother, Lester, warned. "They might be able to hear the blast at the house."

The thought of his father striking out through the woods in search of his wayward son was enough to derail Spike's fireworks display.

Instead, he decided to build a fire.

"Let's see how much smoke we can make out here," he suggested, arranging leaves in a neat pile.

"Bu-but," Lester spoke again. "Don't you think they'll see the smoke back at—?"

Too late. With a quick flick of his wrist, Spike set the pile ablaze.

The experiment proved a roaring success. Flaming leaves, caught by the gentle summer breeze, soon spawned several small ground fires in Grandma Brawley's woods. We all leapt into another fine Sabbath-afternoon activity—fire fighting.

"This one's out!" came a harried cry from the east. From the west a panicky voice said, "Then get over here!" From my recollection of those moments, anyone viewing this scene might have mistaken us for a group of deep-woods religious fanatics practicing a secret ritual dance, the Sabbath firestomp.

Pausing to catch my breath, I glanced up into the trees. *They* were on fire!

The situation seemed too hot for us to handle. "Spike!" I shouted. "You'd better move it to the house and get some help!"

By now Spike sensed that a well-paddled behind would sit better than a stint in the state penitentiary as a full-fledged arsonist. Without looking back, he shot off through the woods to 'fess up and secure assistance.

I have no idea what happened back at Grandma Brawley's

17

house, but I like to imagine Spike's dad sitting in the living room with an interested unchurched dinner guest, talking religion.

"Yes, the book of Revelation says clearly that in the end the wicked will be destroyed by—"

"*Fire!*" Spike screams as he flies into the room, out of breath.

The dinner guest's eyes grow wide. Spike's father's eyes grow narrow. Spike realizes that soon there will be weeping and gnashing of teeth.

Before Spike returned to us, the wail of the volunteer fire department's siren already filled the air. The woods became filled with flurried activity. Most of it came from the firefighters' eventual victory over the flames. But some of it occurred behind a large tree where Spike and his dad had headed off together for a post-fire season of discipline.

All of which leads me to this truism: It's never too late to start making good choices. Nowadays, I spend my Sabbaths doing things that are unlikely to arouse the ire of Smokey the Bear. I trust that my new choices please the One who made the Sabbath a day of delight.

Of course, I would be remiss if I didn't mention the most important choice of all: "Choose for yourselves this day whom you will serve" (Joshua 24:15). Passing up what Jesus has to offer isn't too hot an idea. In fact, as far as I'm concerned, it would be a downright crime.

---

*Both incidents adapted from Donald J. Sobol and Rose Sobol, *Encyclopedia Brown's Book of Strange But True Crimes* (New York: Scholastic, 1991).

Truth Tip #3

Determine Which "Wants" Are Needs

WHEELS OF MISFORTUNE

Cars began driving me crazy at the age of 17, barely into first gear on my journey down the road of experience. Yet a plea of youthful innocence makes insufficient excuse for my overlooking the trouble that loomed ahead. I must now face the hard truth that common sense and consumer savvy took a back seat to the pressing desire of the moment. An accelerating urge cast me into the clutches of that monster known as the "previously-owned car."

Until the Department of Motor Vehicles reluctantly gave me official license to hit the road, I remained fairly content with my primary means of conveyance: a birthday bike my folks had purchased for me at, of all places, a store called Western Auto. But the time had come to put away childish things. I would be upwardly mobile now. Oblivious to what I might get myself into, I let car ownership rank right up there with air, food, and water.

I had already acquired a certain taste in the area of personal motorvation. Unlike some of my horsepower-enamored friends, I was searching for a vehicle that reflected my own personality— pure class.

But just as my quest to obtain a set of wheels was gaining momentum, I heard our pastor quote Matthew 6:19 in a sermon. He said we ought not to depend on things that "moth and rust destroy." That seemed to have a direct bearing on my current ambition.

At first, I thought I could circumvent the problems of this counsel by opting for a leather-upholstered, fiberglass-bodied Corvette. On seeing the average retail price of those beauties, however, I had to abandon that idea. Instead, I chose to put my faith in moth balls and committed to memory the telephone number of the nearest Zeibart dealer.

That summer I labored long and hard to come up with the resources to help make my dream come true. Finally, Dad gave in.

"All right," he said. "If you can find a real deal, I suppose I'll
lend you some cash."

My lobbying had paid off. And Dad certainly didn't need to
worry about my finding a "real deal." I'd know the right car
when I saw it.

As it turned out, a snazzy set of wheels awaited me across
town. A friend of mine knew about an old Lincoln Continental I
"ought to be able to buy cheap."

At this point, I would like to call your attention to a small but
deadly phrase often said by garage-sale addicts and potential
buyers of previously owned automobiles: "I can fix it myself."
Could those same individuals recoup the expenditure set forth
later while they attempt to fulfill this prophecy, the national debt
could be eliminated by late this afternoon.

Having not yet learned the falsehood ensconced within this
thought, I headed over to look at the car. It turned out to be a 1961
model (which at least made it younger than me) and was similar
in body style to its contemporary, the PT boat. The car appeared
in reasonably good shape. At least, there was nothing wrong that
I couldn't fix myself.

The owner fired up the engine, and I gave the entire vehicle a
thorough, all-encompassing glance. Although its sagging tires and
smoky exhaust suggested a less-than-perfect maintenance record,
I convinced myself there was nothing of major concern. So maybe
a '61 Lincoln wasn't much of a threat coming off the stoplight in
town. I was above that. This car would send an unmistakable signal to all potential female passengers that its driver was a knight in
shining sheet metal. Of course, I didn't plan to make a purchase of
this magnitude without first negotiating a little on the price.

"So," I said nonchalantly to the owner, "what do you think a
car like this is worth?"

"Three hundred bucks and you can drive it away," he told me.

I tried not to laugh in his face. Drawing on my shrewd dick-
ering prowess, I said, "I'll take it."

It would be hard to ask for more in my first car, except for
brakes. Even then, they worked most of the time as long as I remembered to fill up the master cylinder with brake fluid every other

day. I forgot to tell Dad about this quirk one morning when we swapped cars. He discovered it for himself shortly before supper.

Upon pulling into the driveway, my unsuspecting father gently applied the stoppers, only to have the pedal sink to the floorboard. Sometime later he managed to bring the car to a halt, choosing the same ground occupied by his utility trailer. I suggested that with some creative steering maneuvers on his part, things might have turned out better. But my appraisal of his driving execution nearly resulted in my own rendezvous with the firing squad. I concluded that I could live with a few extra creases in my fender skirts.

My tenuous relationship with automobiles continued into my twenties. Still single then, I decided the time had come to take action. Perhaps the sleek, aerodynamic design of a European sports car would make up for my own deficiencies of body style, athletic ability, and speed.

I spotted the perfect solution sitting smack in the front row at the local car dealership. Granted, a pre-owned Fiat 850 running flat-out down the side of Mount Everest in a tail wind tops out around 52 miles per day. But it was a convertible, and hopefully the romance of a moonlit night would deter my date from noticing a lack of momentum.

The dealer gave a quick rundown on the car, being honest enough to point out that the convertible top was a little worn.

"That's OK," I said, recalling that I had recently purchased a roll of pre-owned electrical tape at a garage sale. "I can fix that myself." We sealed the deal.

Soon I had completed all the arrangements for an amorous evening under the stars. Pulling out all the stops, I had chosen an intimate little Italian restaurant in a nearby town as our first goal. My date and I had traveled several miles on our journey to Pizza Hut when a fine mist began to gently kiss our shoulders. I cast my lovely rider a longing glance.

"I sure wish you'd put the roof up," she said.

A subtle tease, perhaps? I decided I'd better raise the roof, lest she decide to exercise that option. Pulling over, I yanked the collapsed lid out of its compartment. By now, the stratospheric smooches had turned into sizable drops. With the top securely in place, I hopped back inside.

My date remained dissatisfied. She belonged to the group of people who believe that a raised convertible top ought to reduce the amount of precipitation inside the vehicle by at least 50 percent. I tried to explain that we were now immersed in what sports-car enthusiasts call a "driving rain." Having no choice but to participate, my date let out her heartfelt response that I was all wet.

Then the engine sputtered and died. We coasted to a stop just off the pavement.

"No need to panic," I assured my distressed damsel. "You see, there's a little round black thing that the spark plug wires get plugged into, which sits on top of the engine. Sometimes it gets a little moisture in it, and the engine quits. It's something I can fix myself," I added.

My traveling companion seemed unpersuaded.

"I think it's flooded," she said flatly.

A comment about her lack of mechanical know-how assembled in my mind, but the sight of water lapping at my date's toes silenced it. I realized that her diagnosis was not based on faulty carburetion.

That romantic interlude was a date with disaster. But later she married me anyway.

A stable marriage failed to put an end to my car troubles. Diana and I had agreed upon a pre-owned Oldsmobile Cutlass Supreme, which met my mandatory requirement of a two-door vehicle. Nothing cries out "family man" like a four-door car, and I wasn't quite ready to sport that label.

The old Olds worked pretty well until we took our big trip to Disneyland. In our relative youth we had not learned the universal law that all pre-owned automobiles break down at the most inconvenient spot possible. Say, the Mojave desert.

On the return leg of our excursion, I was basking in the glory of having my picture taken with Mickey and Goofy. But as the miles passed, I grew uneasy over an unfamiliar chortling sound under the hood. I kept my eyes peeled for signs of an exit ramp. On the interstate in the Mojave, exit ramps and icebergs appear with about the same frequency. Happily, we had a ramp sighting just before dusk.

The sign hailing our arrival did little to calm my nerves. On a board, betwixt a hand-painted setting sun and a lone saguaro cactus was the discomforting greeting, "Welcome to Baker, California—Gateway to Death Valley." It was too late to turn back now.

We crept slowly along Main Street in search of a gas station. My wife spotted one on her side of the road. "Baker Fill 'Em Up" would answer our prayers. In bold letters on the side of the building were the words, "24-Hour Wrecker and Repair Service." We both exhaled, certain that we'd be on the road again soon.

Pulling in, I rolled up to the service bay. But as I stepped out of the car, the gigantic garage door began to descend.

"Sorry, we're closed," a well-oiled voice rang out just before the door hit the floor. Apparently it was negotiable as to which 24 hours in any given week "Baker Fill 'Em Up" would devote to the repair and/or wrecking of automobiles.

Further down the street we found a dilapidated diner with a separate three-bay garage on the opposite side of the parking lot. "Death Valley Restaurant and Garage" was our only hope of getting out of town before sundown.

I wheeled in and coasted over to the garage side. Placing the gear shift in neutral, I suggested to Diana that she stay in the car while I investigated.

Inside the fluorescent-lit garage, several locals, RC Colas in hand, were inspecting the boss's new acquisition—an orange Plymouth Road Runner with mag wheels and slick tires. Having been duly congratulated by "the boys," the bearded and mustachioed boss turned to me.

"What do you need?" he asked almost without moving his lips.

I explained that our car seemed to have some sort of indigestion, and I'd appreciate it if somebody could have a look at it. The main man turned to his crew.

"Clayton," he said to one greaser standing behind a rolling tool chest. "Take a trouble light out to this fella's car and see what ya can see."

The unshaven, T-shirt-clad toolie ambled slowly over to a workbench and picked up a wrench. Clayton had to amble slowly, I noticed, because his right leg was encased in a hip-to-ankle cast. He removed an extension cord and a light from a hook on the wall. I followed him out to our car, a little apprehensive.

"Fire it up and pop the hood, would ya?" he said. Precisely at this point I picked up the scent of impending doom. Judging from the whiff of booze on his breath, this mechanic favored solving problems with a few Screwdrivers.

Caught between a rock and a hard liquor drinker, I asked my wife to start the motor and pull the hood release. I watched helplessly as the inebriate fumbled around in the vicinity of the engine. He stumbled from one side of the car to the other, apparently searching for some elusive part. The soused grease monkey finally admitted, "I cain't seem to find the bolt to set the timing."

I, the walking mechanical failure, pointed out to him the object of his search on my side of the distributor cap.

"Why, sure enough, there it is," he replied. Relieved to have discovered its whereabouts, he set about to loosen the bolt. So difficult did this prove to be that his vocabulary soon matched our car's exterior—metallic blue.

By now I was losing my expectation that we would leave Baker with a smoother-running vehicle. In an attempt to spare the bungler any further embarrassment, I offered to pay him for his "trouble" and move along. Thankfully, he did not respond to this blow to his ego with a greasy knuckle sandwich.

"You can do what you want," he said with a sneer, slamming the hood shut. "All I know is one thing." No doubt he hadn't memorized the Alcoholic's Anonymous creed. "The next town is a long, lonely stretch of road away."

Even as he spoke, a shiver ran up my spine. The next locale of any consequence was Las Vegas, a hundred miles to the northeast. Should I take the gamble? I reasoned that our odds of making it there were better than actually getting this gassed-up garage guy to fix our car. Fortunately, my bet paid off.

Today I drive a very basic pre-owned automobile. Four wheels. Four cylinders. Four doors (*yecch*). Finally my car makes a statement that rings true: "Herein drives a basic guy." Arriving at a given point has become more important to me than driving one home.

Sure, my heart still flutters at the sight of a restored '55 T-Bird. But the counsel of a certain Man regarding such moth-and-rust-ridden non-necessities helps keep things in perspective. That and the fact that I'm usually broke. Now there's something I haven't been able to fix myself.

Truth
Tip #4

Give It
Your
Best Shot

BROTHERS AND CISTERN

My father, a certified public accountant by profession, has always been a farmer at heart. Unable to control his enthusiasm for manual labor, Dad decided one summer that the time had come to introduce his adolescent offspring to some honest work.

"I think you two boys ought to contribute a little more to this family," he informed us one evening. David and I tried to convince him that we had already given at the office, but he didn't buy our little philanthropic fabrication. It appeared that carefree summer mornings on the shores of *Gilligan's Island* would soon be a memory.

My father *did,* however, manage to stimulate our interest by announcing a plan he had devised whereby we could become independently wealthy before school began again in the fall. The secret ingredient in this sure-fire recipe for success: cucumbers.

"The way I see it," our enterprising dad elaborated, "we could make better use of that empty field out back. The taxes put too much of a strain on the family budget." Something told me the strain would shift to other areas shortly.

Dad looked straight at his two "lazy boys" plopped in the overstuffed chairs named for them. The TV blared in the background. As a sinister grin crossed his face, he added with relish, "And since there's nothing *on* that land, we might as well put something *in* it. Right?"

My brother and I glanced uneasily at each other.

He continued, "If we start getting the soil worked up tomorrow, we should be ready to plant by the end of the week."

From then on, the crew of the *U.S.S. Minnow* would have to go it alone. We were about to get shipped off to work.

Actually, planting the seeds didn't strike me as difficult.

Thinking about the misery they would soon bring bothered us, though. As Dad worked beside us during the long twilight hours, he offered us encouraging words like, "Only 97 more rows to go," and, "To make your work a little easier, I bought you both new hoes at the hardware store today." Hardly our idea of a labor-saving device, but a valiant attempt to bolster our sagging spirits nonetheless.

He saved the best announcement for a grand finale. "One thing's certain," he said. "Those empty 5-gallon paint buckets I've been saving will come in mighty handy for hauling water out here to this field."

Surely he jests, I thought to myself. *Has my level-headed accountant father lost his mental balance?* The closest water faucet stuck out of the side of our house a good two acres away! Exercise was one thing, but this was going too far.

My apprehension eased slightly as Dad explained that we'd use a flatbed trailer hitched to his pride and toy, a 1947 Ford tractor, to transport the overflowing water buckets. But even this innovative approach wouldn't save much time. *There's another way to water these cucumbers,* I thought.

I recalled seeing The Professor on *Gilligan's Island* rig up a bicycle-powered water system. While Gilligan pedaled furiously, a bamboo pipeline carried water directly to where it was needed. Maybe it would work for us, too.

However, the state of Michigan has never ranked high as a producer of bamboo. Add to that my uncanny propensity for catching my pant leg in my bicycle chain. The Professor's pedal-pumper idea got the heave-ho.

After a few days, the cucumber plants began to poke their heads out of the ground. The green sprouts would expect a drink before long. I came up with another idea to save us from the water bucket blues.

"You know," I said to David, "I think what we need here is a cistern."

My brother looked a little confused and asked, "You want to have a girl come in and water the plants for us?"

"No, no," I said. "A cistern is what people in ancient times called a well. In the Bible, Joseph's brothers threw him into a cistern. That's where I learned about it. It's just a big hole in the

29

ground that you fill up with water. It'd be the perfect thing for our cucumber patch."

"Hey, that might not be a bad idea," David said. Pointing to a far corner of the field he added, "We could put it over there in that low spot. It's already kind of swampy, and the cistern would probably get full real quick."

"Right," I agreed. "And just think of all the time we'll end up saving! But let's not tell anybody about it, especially Dad. It'll be a surprise!"

The following morning, lacking the soundness of mind to realize the amount of work involved in digging an open well, we grabbed a couple of shovels and set out for the sight.

Working on and off at the project over the next two days, we scooped our way toward China. As the pit got deeper, the soil became more moist. Encouraged at the prospects, I lowered myself over the side and kept digging. I was really getting into it now.

The following afternoon, we declared the well officially dug. We had reached the formidable depth of six feet.

Figuring that our fresh creation would need a little time to get its grow-lotion in motion, we decided to wait until the next day to test the waters. That way, we reasoned, it would have enough time to collect a goodly amount of fluid. We hit the sack dreaming of a water wonderland.

Arising bright and early, we made our way to the cucumber patch and headed to the well. Peering slowly into the pit, I let out a whoop of delight.

"We've got water!" I yelled. My brother looked for himself. It was true! A pool of brown water lay peacefully in the bottom of our new ancient well.

"We did it!" I shouted. "Just wait till Dad sees this!"

"Boy," David said a little apprehensively, "the water looks kind of dirty, doesn't it?"

"Oh, that's OK," I said. "Plants grow in dirt, don't they? They won't mind a little extra nourishment. Come on, let's try it out!"

Grabbing a 5-gallon bucket, I bent over and drew out a pail full of water from our reservoir. Together we drenched some of the plants with the root-beer-colored liquid.

"Are you sure they'll be able to drink this stuff?" David asked.

"Stop worrying," I reassured him. "Water is water. Besides, if these cukes get thirsty enough, they'll drink anything."

"I sure hope you're right."

Soon we had depleted the well of its meager resources. Knowing that more would appear if we waited, we decided to take a Popsicle break. We figured by the time we got back, the cistern would have refilled.

Upon our return, however, we discovered that the healthy cucumber seedlings we had watered now resembled chocolate-covered cacti. The plants sported a thick brown coat of dry mud, apparently a dirty trick played on us by the hot summer sun. Suddenly the sweet taste of success had gone sour. We were in a real pickle.

Keeping our few wits about us, we searched for survivors. Realizing that it was possible the mud hadn't had enough time to finish its dastardly deed, we ran back to the house and filled a couple of buckets with clear water. We sped back to the scene of the grime and began CPR—"cleaning the plants' remains"—by gently bathing their leaves, hoping somehow the injured would respond. We had to try to fix everything before Dad got home. We didn't want to be held responsible for the world's first cukeular explosion.

Happily, most of the wounded did manage to pull through. We went on to pick many a cucumber off those very plants.

Looking back, I believe that even if our experiment had failed, we still would have returned to school richer than before. Winston Churchill once said, "Success is never final, failure is never fatal; it is courage that counts." Although we didn't realize it, Dad had provided us with soil fertile enough for our own growth, along with the cucumbers. We tapped more than just water. We felt the satisfaction of action. At least our well was done, even if we hadn't done it too well.

Truth
Tip #5

Believe in Your Father's Love

> "HOW GREAT IS THE LOVE THE FATHER HAS LAVISHED ON US,
> THAT WE SHOULD BE CALLED THE CHILDREN OF GOD!"
> (1 JOHN 3:1).

BABY DAZE

Someone once said, "Our lives are ordered by the consequences of defining moments." Actually, I said that. I figure nobody will ever quote me on anything, so I'd better attend to it myself.

I can recall many defining moments that have changed the course of my life, including the time I was apprehended after exiting a sixth-grade art class through the rear window. But nothing, and I mean *nothing*, ordered the rest of my living moments like the words, "We're going to have a baby."

My wife chose just the right moment to gently share the news with me. Diana informed me of the impending blessed event then hoisted me from the floor and asked what I thought of the whole idea.

"Our lives are ordered by the consequences of defining moments," I said.

Notice that my wife inadvertently employed the plural subject "we" in announcing the forthcoming milestone. Ah, but this *is* correct. No longer does the expectant mother fly solo into a colorless operating room and emerge hours later with a brand-spanking-new infant for Dad to admire. No, no, *n-o-o*. In this age of pastel-toned, oak-trimmed birthing suites, *we* have a baby.

And so, as a public service, I submit to the reader the following compendium of proven tips for making one's way through the baby daze, that time of life when your little loved one dominates your entire existence.

Choosing a name

Tradition dictates that parents select a name for their new offspring, since a number alone lacks a certain personal touch.

"Honey, would you please change 34920's diaper?" (The polite response to this is, of course, "No, thank you.") About the only place where a number-name proves effective is the state prison system, not a life goal any parent worth his credentials would hope to see his kid achieve.

Many couples consider naming the baby after a close loved one or other significant other (I'm hearing an echo in this chapter). Bear in mind, though, that certain names have lost their contemporary feel. For example, naming your child Matilda Louise or Mortimer Henry may put the youngster at risk of verbal abuse during roll call on the first day of kindergarten.

A spouse may wish to pay tribute by naming the baby after a parent. While this is acceptable to some, it may necessitate wearing a bulletproof vest while visiting the parent whose name you *did not* choose.

Finally, consider consulting a baby name book at your local library. These amazing volumes contain perhaps 10,000 names, not one of which you and your spouse can agree upon.

The birthing class

No, this is not some sociologist's bungling attempt to lump all expectant parents into one group. Rather, here one masters the skill of mind over body, with the main goal of preventing injury to the father and the supporting cast in the delivery room.

During labor the mother controls pain by "regulated breathing patterns." The two of you repeat such meaningful phrases as "Huh-huh-huh" and "Hoo-hoo-hoo" while the adjacent computer monitor provides visual evidence of a contraction approximating 28.9 on the Richter scale. I note from personal experience that the "Ha-ha-ha!" breathing pattern does not facilitate bonding between husband and wife during this experience.

Upon your graduation from the birthing class, it is appropriate to celebrate. I suggest a good night's sleep, since you will not have one for several months after the baby arrives.

The delivery

Like George Washington, the father of the U.S.A., this dad cannot tell a lie. The hard truth is that the hours preceding the delivery of our first baby were filled with a mixture of gut-wrenching moans and unabashed screams of anguish. My wife wasn't doing so well either.

I took courage, however, in trusting that when the time was right, our baby *would* appear. Finally, our new son showed his face, something, I might add, that I would hardly describe as a sight for sore eyes. Thankfully, a proficient RN swabbed his countenance clean and diapered his rear deck—but not before baby paid his first "deposit," unfortunately for the delivering physician.

We turn now to life after the hospital zone. The following information is vital for the survival of new parents, also known as zombies.

Receiving the bill(s)

Parents should not be surprised to discover several envelopes filling their mailbox approximately 10 seconds after they pull into the driveway with their new baby. Be prepared for the steady outpouring of bills to continue for somewhere around, say, six years.

Be sure to sit down while reading these communiqués. The uninitiated may find himself or herself growing faint upon learning that hospital aspirins go for five bucks apiece. Yet I ask new parents to bear in mind that hospitals cannot do business for free. Do you think they get those little nut cups for the aspirins for nothing? Really, folks.

Another hospital-bill phenomenon: You receive bills from not only the attending physician, but from other entities and persons like assorted laboratories and Move It Along Midwifery, Inc. (catchy motto: "We Deliver"). You may also discover an invoice bearing the corporate address of Peruvian Adhesive and Yams. The good folks down at PAY manufacture the stick-um that keeps your bill envelopes sealed so very securely until they arrive at your home. (They also have a contract to supply the hospital cafeteria with the primary ingredient required for item four on the menu, Chef Sam's Really Different-tasting Yams.)

Try to keep your spirits high with the thought that these bills eventually come to an end. To maintain a sense of financial security during this period, you may wish to block out the thought that by the time Junior is ready for college, tuition will have risen to about half a million dollars per semester.

Responding to questions

Upon toting home your bundle of joy, you will hear endless questions from well-meaning friends, local and distant relatives, and gawking supermarket shoppers. Prepare your responses in advance. Following are some Frequently Asked Questions (FAQs) new parents face.

"Is it a boy or a girl?" An irritating query, given that your little blanketful of femininity is dressed head-to-toe in gender-correct pink. Nevertheless, in such a situation it is critical that you resist all temptation to respond with a direct "It's a girl, *ma'am.*" Although you may gain momentary satisfaction from this unchristian barb, the large gentleman to whom you have directed this witticism may view it as an invitation to do you great bodily harm.

"Is the baby on a schedule yet?" Actually, each of our children was exemplary in the matter of regular sleeping and feeding times. They would awake like clockwork every hour on the hour between sunset and dawn, wailing as if they'd been deprived of nutrition for the past six weeks.

Discussion on this question usually terminates with the mumbling of, "If only someone would volunteer to baby-sit little Cryanna for a few hours . . ."

"Did you have a long labor?" First come to an agreement on the definition of "long." You'll find a variety of beliefs as to what constitutes a long labor. Your obstetrician will likely designate anything over 12 hours, while the typical mother probably considers anything over 12 seconds a *very long* labor.

Ironically, while the average mother does not view this section of the birth experience as the epitome of pleasure, the theme comes up often and at length among those who have personally endured it. Thankfully, I cannot include myself in this group, so I would be remiss in attempting to suggest a credible response to the question.

"Are you planning to have another one?" This corresponds to asking a recovering mugging victim whether he intends to make a career goal out of night-time graffiti removal in Central Park. Timing is everything, and anyone positing this question of a new mother should have a very good time in the 100-yard dash.

All told, life in the baby lane sometimes seems to lead you toward insanity. That's why it's so astonishing that we wouldn't trade it for a free shopping spree in the U.S. Mint factory outlet store. Some things money just can't buy, and what we've learned about love during the baby daze is one of those things. If two people, amidst such a mass of dirty diapers and sleepless nights, can form a love for their child that is stronger than steel, imagine how our heavenly Father must feel toward us! Unconditional, undeserved, unabashed *love.*

Wouldn't you know it, I hear the distant cry of a discontented neonate. Another chance to strengthen the father-son bond. Do I have a volunteer for just *one* night of baby-sitting?

Truth Tip #6

Admit Your Mistakes

"We have sinned, we have done wrong"
(Daniel 9:15).

What's *Your* Excuse?

If there were a National Gallery of Stupid Excuses, these gems would surely find a home there:

"No, Mom, I'll just stay here in front of the TV all day. I'm too sick to see a doctor."

"Sorry I didn't have time to do my report on the whachacallit woodpecker, Professor Birdlove. I've been really busy sleeping and stuff."

"But I *need* more allowance, Dad. I want to buy a Dr. Waterspout computerized heat-seeking squirt gun. It'll be good for my eye/hand coordination."

"Spend our vacation with you on a yacht cruise, headed for a remote island in the South Pacific? We'd love to but, uh, we really wanted to try something relaxing this year."

"Aw, I'm too beat to do any more laps, Coach Brawn," followed by, "C'mon, Tyler, last one to the locker room is a Texas fruitcake!"

And so forth.

In this world you will find about as many stupid excuses as there are stupid excusees. Not that a person must have an IQ in the minus range to offer a stupid excuse. Even the most brilliant among us have endured a temporary brain power outage.

One fine spring day my pal Tomahawk Stiles and I could stand it no longer. Opening day of baseball season had arrived, yet we were chained to desks in English class, ripping sentences apart and putting them back together. As I searched in vain for a misplaced modifier, I was struck by a stroke of genius: Why not create our own little Astrodome right in the school hallway between classes?

"Sounds good to me," Tomahawk mumbled, struggling to solve his grammar problem. "Let's see now, what's best? 'The dog *drove* Ricardo to the vet' or 'Ricardo *was driven* to the vet by the dog'"? Before I could offer my opinion, the bell out in right field . . . er . . . the hall . . . sounded. Forget nouns and verbs and dangling participles—for the next seven minutes it was time to "Play ball!"

"Want the plate or the mound?" I asked Tomahawk, grabbing gloves and ball from our locker.

"Catcher. You can practice your new pitch. What d'ya call it?"

"Atomic curve. OK, you watch out for teachers—I gotta concentrate on the strike zone." Moving out of mainstream traffic, we set up at opposite ends of the hallway. Tomahawk assumed his position, and I focused on my catcher. Finally, he gave me the signal for the atomic curve.

"Throw me the atomic curve!" he yelled. (Hardly effective against an opposing player, we abandoned the screaming signal technique before actually taking the field that season.)

Winding up, I flung the pill mightily toward Tomahawk. But with the ball about halfway to its intended recipient, it switched to slow motion. In my mind's eye I can still see that sphere sailing lazily, though purposefully, down the hall, narrowly missing Laura Jenson and her clique of fashion fawns . . . and Tomahawk's outstretched Carlton Fisk autographed glove.

To this day the sound of shattering glass—the type they put in school doors—makes both my hairs stand on end. Of course I'm kidding—about my hair count, not the busted door. We're talking Damages R Us.

As if he had beamed down from the *USS Enterprise*, our math teacher, Mr. Greenwood, appeared magically on the scene.

"Atomic curve," Tomahawk said sheepishly to the scowling number-cruncher.

Mr. Greenwood seemed unmoved by my catcher's explanation. Instead, he asked us to remove our gloves, then escorted us upstairs to the general manager's office. It didn't take long for the boss to make his position on the matter clear: Playing hall-ball seemed about as intelligent as running the Boston marathon in high heels.

As the principal wound up to pronounce final judgment on us, possible routes out of this mess raced through my mind:

1. I could bring a signed note from Mom:

"Dear Principal,

Please excuse my son from smashing the school door into a thousand tiny pieces by hurling his atomic curveball through it. He meant no harm.

Signed,

His Mom"

Yeah, sure. Mom refused to sign a note for me to skip school to watch the National League playoffs. No way would she cover me for a broken school door.

2. I could skip the rest of eighth grade and get a job. Then it hit me: A job would involve work. There had to be an easier way.

3. I could blame it on Tomahawk. I'd get out of it, and he'd get over it—eventually. Then I realized that before my pal would extend the gift of forgiveness to me he'd likely pound me into the ground like a fencepost. I felt a headache coming on.

4. I could scold the principal and school planners for not having the foresight to put the door three feet to the west of its present location. Or . . .

5. I could stop making excuses, bear up to the responsibility, accept the consequences—and think ahead next time. Not fun, but at least I wouldn't have to worry about my story hanging together (or someone stringing up barbed wire on me). I decided the best "excuse" was the truth.

The atomic curveball turned out to be a pretty explosive topic at the dinner table that evening. But after I received notice of the termination of the appropriate privilege—no allowance until I had paid for the door—I realized I still had two important things left: my best friend, and a very comfortable conscience. Both of which are worth a great deal indeed.

Truth
Tip #7

Think
Lose/win

Born Loser

Wallet. Shoes. Self-respect. You name it, and I've probably lost it. "I Found It" bumper stickers remain an abstract concept to me. I'm a born loser.

But my rise to fame as a loser reached its zenith the day I lost the tractor.

Still a mere youth, I had landed a job as a residential environmental maintenance specialist—I cleaned up apartments after renters moved out. In addition I carried the responsibilities of staff "gofer"—go fer this and go fer that. So when the boss called me to his office for a special assignment one day, I wondered whether he wanted a glazed doughnut or a long-john.

Now, Mr. Stevens' office did not look like most offices I'd seen. It resembled a pool hall. A swag light hung low over his desk, and plush carpet covered the floor. Mr. Stevens had stepped out for a moment, and as I walked in I pictured myself behind the desk. There I sat, leaning back in my leather, button-tufted executive chair, feet propped comfortably on the blotter. With a savvy smile on my face, I slowly reached for my pen and signed the contract closing another multi-million-dollar apartment deal. Then I sent Mr. Stevens out for a long-john.

I jerked back to reality as the door rattled behind me, and Mr. Stevens walked around to his desk. "Sorry to keep you waiting, son, but you know how it is in the millionaire business. But then again, I guess you wouldn't know."

True.

He continued. "It's like this, son. I got a call from the Rose Hill complex. They're having some sort of problem with their lawn tractor. Now, normally I wouldn't get involved in this type of thing; I'd rather leave it to the maintenance crew. But we're in a bind this time. The renters are getting restless over the height of their grass. That's where you come in."

I stood up straight. Maybe today I'd get that lucky break I needed. Undoubtedly Mr. Stevens planned to test me somehow, to see if I could handle greater responsibility.

"I'm at your service, Mr. Stevens," I saluted.

He put his hand on my shoulder. "Son," he said, "I'd like you to take my own John Deere lawn tractor over to the Rose Hill complex. I usually don't lend out my personal property, but I'll make an exception this time. I brought my tractor from home this morning, and I didn't have time to take it to Rose Hill. I had a meeting—you know how it is in the millionaire . . . oh, forget it. It's already on the trailer. All you have to do is make sure it's chained down tight and hitch it up to the company van. I'll let them know you're on your way. Good luck, son."

With an abrupt "about face" I marched out to the company parking lot where the van and trailer were parked.

Before long I had the trailer hooked up. Checking the chains that held the tractor down, I decided they'd hold for the short distance to Rose Hill. Besides that, my 130-pound hulk of a frame only allowed for so much tightening.

I climbed into the van and checked the side-mounted mirrors. They didn't spread far enough to let me see the trailer behind the van. Windowless back doors didn't help matters. But I wasn't going very far. Pulling onto Highway 31, I thought about how impressed Mr. Stevens would be.

A few miles from the Rose Hill apartment complex I heard a car honking and someone yelling behind my van. I looked in my mirror. *That's odd*, I said to myself. *I don't believe I know those people.*

A mile or so farther down the road the same two guys floored it and began to pass me. Pulling up even with my van, they rolled down a window. "Hey, buddy!" one guy yelled. "You lost that tractor back there about a mile!" They laughed and roared off.

I felt sick. My heart began to palpitate, and my life passed before my eyes. I knew that I would shortly die.

Maybe they were joking. I stuck my head far out the window and looked behind. No joke. Just an empty trailer. I had lost Mr. Stevens' tractor!

I jerked the steering wheel around and changed course from

45

east to west. *How could this happen to me?* I questioned. *I had so much to live for . . .*

As I retraced my path, I scrutinized the roadside, trying to catch a glimpse of my lost cargo. *Maybe it won't be as bad as I think,* I comforted myself. *Maybe it landed on its wheels and just sort of gently bounced until it stopped.*

Just then I caught sight of a large mass of green-and-yellow debris on someone's front lawn. It appeared to have been, at one time, a John Deere lawn tractor. Pulling the van onto the shoulder of the road, I slowly got out, clinging to the hope that by some stroke of good fortune I might be standing on a fault line and the earth would suddenly open up and swallow me alive.

I strolled around the remains but saw little I could do. Rigor mortis had set in. The tractor's hood was smashed, its front wheel completely severed. I began to imagine that I would look this way soon after I got back to Mr. Stevens' office.

Realizing that standing there staring would not resurrect the thing, I somehow managed to maneuver the customized John Deere tractor back onto the trailer. I then drove off to face the dreaded music.

The final movements came rapidly. Mr. Stevens told me with a certain note in his voice that he would always look at our relationship as a "learning experience." Then he fired me. He apparently reasoned that since I had lost *his* tractor, I should lose *my* job.

Over the long haul, I, like Mr. Stevens, have learned something about "losers." It seems there is at least one occasion when "losing" is a winning proposition:

> "He who finds his life will lose it, and he
> who loses his life for my sake will find it"
> (Matthew 10:39, RSV).

That's especially comforting to a *reborn* loser.

Truth
Tip #8

Defeat Deceit

"A MAN OF PERVERSE HEART DOES NOT PROSPER; HE WHOSE TONGUE IS DECEITFUL FALLS INTO TROUBLE" (PROVERBS 17:20).

FAKEBITE!

Drill sergeants and children share a disturbing characteristic: they both demand a great deal of attention.

I might have followed the lead of Gomer Pyle as one of America's best, but the Marine Corps, exhibiting true military intelligence, forbids the enlistment of nine-year-old combatants. So I joined the ranks of attention-seeking children.

My limited experience had already taught me how few opportunities arise to practice undisguised self-centeredness. One occasion, however, provided me a chance to satisfy my desire for others to notice me—the annual church picnic.

That year the picnic committee had decided on Riverview Park as the perfect spot for an afternoon of fellowship and festivities. Here men, women, and children were afforded an obstructed view of a complete chemical waste transportation system. In days past this was known as a river. Church picnickers could munch a bunch of Fritos while watching an endless variety of water-borne toxic debris drifting lazily by.

Of course, we youngsters thought nothing of adult concerns like environmental hazards. After a healthy dose of corn chips and potato salad, and a "minor league" ball game (we were all minors), most of us boys decided to cool off in the murky mess flowing nearby. Shortly the sounds of carefree summer frolicking filled the air.

"Watch out for this broken beer bottle over here."

"Hey, what's this brick doing in the water?"

"I just saw a snake!"

A snake? I didn't actually walk on water, but a couple of seconds later I was standing on the bank, urging my colleagues to be courageous.

A group of concerned picnickers gathered around to witness

the spectacle. Questions and commentary came rapid-fire from the crowd.

"How long was it?" Mr. Wilson asked.

"I'm not really sure," his son Micky said, still standing in the water. "It was moving real fast!"

"I've heard there are water moccasins in this part of the river," another person chimed in.

I'm no herpetologist, but I was pretty sure water moccasins were not shoes especially designed for performing miraculous feats on water.

Finally, Mr. Wilson, apparently not convinced there was real danger, told Micky that if he saw the snake sneaking back into our swimming area he should just leave it alone. "It won't bite anybody unless you give it a reason to," he said.

Soon afterward, Dad gave the "homeward bound" command, but I was slow in getting to the car. My mind was pondering the possibilities the snake scenario might afford.

Snakebite, huh? It would make quite an impact on my friends and family if they thought I had actually been bitten—specially by a water moccasin.

I envisioned Dad kneeling at the foot of my deathbed.

"Son, can you ever forgive me for the many times I unjustly administered the board of correction to you?" he said, his eyes full of sorrow.

Mom wept openly as she admitted the injustice of asking me to perform unreasonable and slavish tasks like picking up my clothes. But still I lay prone.

Then the door gently opened, and Amanda Walker entered. Between sobs, she gasped out,"If only I'd had a chance to tell him how much I cared. I was even going to sit next to him on the bus tomorrow."

The plan was a go-ahead. But I would have to make it look good.

Plopping myself comfortably in the rear seat of the car, I waved goodbye to my buddies. They had no idea of the dramatic events about to unfold within the four doors of our family sedan.

As Dad wheeled onto the main road, I knew my time had come. Slowly bringing my knee up toward my face, I closed my eyes and opened my mouth. In a remarkable display of senselessness, but determined to make an impression, I bit down on my right kneecap.

Judging from the blinding pain, I felt confident that my immediate goal had been accomplished.

"*Yeoooww!*" I grabbed my indented knee.

Had a police helicopter been flying overhead at the time, the pilot's eyes would have popped their sockets at my father's theatrical whipping of the car from side to side on the two-lane road.

"What's the matter!?" Dad cried in ear-damaging decibels.

Too scrupulous to tell an out-and-out lie, I whimpered and pointed to the well-embedded tooth marks adorning my knobby kneecap. Then, in an honest attempt to lead Mom and Dad down a path of gross deception, I said, "Well, I didn't actually *see* the snake . . ."

Mom's face turned reptilian green.

"Maybe a water moccasin . . ." I added with a moan.

Dad pulled the car over to the side of the road then peered over the rear seat and studied my knee. Although I was reasonably sure he had bought the story hook and line, his face registered a small sinker of doubt. Eyes narrowed, he leaned in closer and surveyed my wound.

"You know," he said, stroking his chin, "it occurs to me that most people who are bitten by a snake feel it right away, not ten minutes after the fact." He looked at Mom. "This is truly a one-of-a-kind phenomenon, wouldn't you agree?"

A light of understanding seemed to dawn upon Mom. I squirmed, sensing some cracks developing in the foundation of my fib.

"But," Dad continued, "there's something not quite right about this bite. And I think I know what it is."

My little sweat glands began pumping big-time perspiration. I knew that silent prayer would be inappropriate. Perhaps Dad might see fit to make this our little secret.

But, pointing to the indentations on my knee, he went on. "It's the way these tooth marks are laid out," he explained. His convicting gaze rose to meet my guilt-ridden face. "As nearly as I can tell," Dad said, "if the 'snake' that bit you were to grin real big, he'd have a gap between his two front teeth that perfectly matches that of someone I happen to know personally."

Pausing for effect, he finished his examination by adding, "Need I say more?" (Scholars translate this ancient saying as,

"Thy goose has been cooked.")

I looked up at Mom then down at the bite. How could I have overlooked the obvious? In my haste to fake the snake, I had not considered that I inherited my grandpa Covault's irregular incisors. My two front teeth made Bugs Bunny's grinders look like dental perfection. For the first time I wished I'd spent more time in the dentist's chair. But that was all fluoride under the bridge now.

Lifting my head again, I looked at Dad and showed him a lip-parting, angelic smile. Perhaps a heart-rending look of innocence would provoke a sympathetic response. I realized too late that my beaming countenance revealed the crowning evidence of my guilt.

I thought perhaps my parents would see an element of humor in the situation. They did not. Mom's face might have been mistaken for a traffic signal, it had become so bright red.

My desire for stardom had vanished. The possibility of lumbering off with my father to the rear of the woodshed became my focus of concern. I knew that if Dad chose to exercise that option he'd make an impact on me that would far surpass any attention-getting gimmick I might conjure up. Confession seemed good for the soul, not to mention another part of me.

"Well, it wasn't exactly a snake . . ." I admitted.

"Something more akin to a *sneak*, perhaps?" Dad suggested.

"Could be," I replied solemnly.

Dad spelled out the down-side to creating such a false impression in some detail. My heartfelt repentance helped grace to prevail over punishment, an outcome that was deeply appreciated on my end.

I haven't been back to Riverview Park for a while, though the memory of that fakeful day lives on in my nightmares. I learned that you shouldn't sink your teeth into falsehood. It brings you way too much 'tention.

Truth Tip #9

Keep Looking Up

> "NOW WE KNOW THAT IF THE EARTHLY TENT WE LIVE IN IS
> DESTROYED, WE HAVE A BUILDING FROM GOD,
> AN ETERNAL HOUSE IN HEAVEN"
> (2 CORINTHIANS 5:1).

MOVING TESTIMONY

Since our marriage began, Diana and I have had many moving experiences. I'm sure we have moved more times than the cursor on my computer screen. If we live in one town for over a year we begin showing signs of *residophobia,* fear of staying in one place too long.

Not that we have *wanted* to move so often. But it is uncanny how an empty bank account causes one to consider taking up serious employment, even if it involves setting the Guinness world record for stuffing a car with one's personal belongings.

We spend the weeks prior to a move gathering cardboard containers for packing. Rummaging through every dumpster in town carries with it the potential for misunderstanding, but you can't allow this to become a concern. You think of nothing but securing approximately one million boxes before the moving truck will arrive next Tuesday.

In the matter of box gathering, I pass on a cognitive technique that will help you maintain a positive outlook: View the process as a treasure hunt. You'll become involved in exchanges like this one on a regular basis:

"My love, guess what I found at Safeway today!"

"I can hardly wait to hear, my sweetest!"

"A large-size Charmin and two banana boxes, complete with handholds!"

"Can it be true? Yes, it must be—even now I smell the scent of rotting fruitskins on your hands! Yet, my love, your joy is only a shadow of my own, for today I discovered something exceedingly wonderful behind 'Nutty' Bolton's Hardware Store: a double-wall air-conditioner box, with the bubble wrap *still in it!*"

"I reel at the very thought, my dearest!"

Unless you have experienced it personally, you can't comprehend the satisfaction that accompanies such finds.

Next comes filling these containers with your household goods. Diana has perfected the Kitchen Dish Paper Wrap method, wherein she delicately bundles each and every plate, cup, and saucer in paper toweling, only stopping short, at my insistence, of sewing name and telephone number into their collars in case the little tykes should become lost. I, on the other hand, consider myself a master of the Garage Tool Toss 'n' Stuff technique. I throw everything within the sound of my voice into a box, then mash it down with a few well-placed stomps for final closure. The Toss 'n' Stuff also works well when the moving crew, hoping to make Wichita by 10:00 that night, stands around watching while you finish packing.

We made our first cross-country move when I accepted a position as a youth pastor. For a couple of years we'd been living in an old house in Michigan, out in the "sticks." The house featured an indoor waterfall that descended from the ceiling into strategically located buckets each time it rained. This we would miss. Could Seattle, with its majestic mountains and beautiful Puget Sound, furnish us with anything as wondrous? Yet we must heed the call.

Miraculously, and I have seen this miracle happen more than once, the driver of the moving truck performed a 370-degree turn that brought the vehicle's rear doors into perfect alignment with our front door. All this while avoiding what was left of the house's gutters, along with the front lamppost and the low-hanging branches of a colorful assortment of trees.

A few hours later, the van stood fully loaded. How the crew managed to accomplish this without employing the Toss 'n' Stuff technique I still do not know. Perhaps they've discovered an even more effective method than mine.

As the moving van disappeared down the road, we returned to the house to do a final walk-through, checking that we'd removed every microscopic piece of dust that might prevent the return of our rental deposit. Satisfied that open-heart surgery could safely be performed in the front hall closet, we strolled out and squeezed into our overstuffed, filled-to-the-gills automobile.

Actually, our car contained more than met the eye. The casual observer would not know that beneath the front seat lay two prone, partially tranquilized felines. Add to them yet another cat, a dog, a pregnant wife, and me—the captain of this unstately ship—and you can guess that we felt somewhat less comfortable than a millipede with bunions. The only fact we rejoiced about was that the temperature had not risen to 100 degrees outside, though it was getting close.

We'd made plans to start early in the day, so at 1:00 that afternoon we pointed our vehicle out the driveway to face our first appointment: dropping off one of our much-loved cats at the Humane Society. Seattle might have something to offer us, but not much to a country cat like Tigger. After we had done the deed, Diana and I hugged each other, christening our Ford Tempo with our tears.

Our first destination was Minneapolis, via the Windy City. But when we hit Chicago, we discovered more than wind. After torrential rains, a section of the road we were traveling on had become as congested as a pollen-filled nasal passage.

Not to worry! I'd learned my way around Shytown. We could just ease off I-294 and slip onto I-290—they both proceeded where I needed to go.

But the best of plans get washed away, and this was what had happened to several of the connecting routes off I-294. We learned the real reason for the slow traffic: The authorities had closed nearby exit ramps to prevent folks from unwittingly becoming submarines upon departing the interstate.

I must say I found it somewhat humorous to observe people parking along the roadway and then hopping over guardrails as they dashed madly on foot toward O'Hare airport to catch planes. I chortled inwardly, however, lest my wide smile become the target of an angry ticket-holder's stylish carry-on bag.

But what of our own situation? Not to worry! I proposed that we simply go full-speed straight ahead, proving to these incapacitated city-dwellers that we country bumpkins knew how to handle this kind of crisis. And so we pushed forward, at about 3 miles per hour, for a very, *very* long time. Happily, the rain had stopped. Unhappily, so had our air conditioner.

Now to worry! Tranquilized cats under the front seats is one thing, *broiled, dead* cats is quite another. Having finally made it through the heart of the disaster area, I decided we'd have to exit and find a service station to fix our conked-out cooler.

We located a repair shop. After a brief diagnosis, a smiling mechanic brought us the glad tidings.

"I can't fix this thing."

"Fine, fine," I said, beaming back. "Thanks for adding the frosting to our little cake of misery."

Knowing we still had 500 miles to go before our day was done, I began looking for a west-bound on-ramp to the interstate. But the city planners, anticipating that one day a depressed young pastoral intern and his pregnant wife with two cats and a dog would be in this very predicament, had thoughtfully avoided constructing a road like that anywhere in the area.

"No problem," I said, smiling through clenched teeth. "I'll take an east-bound on-ramp. We'll surely find a way to get back on the other side before we reach the watery mess we've just spent much of our wedded life passing through."

Later that day, as we again approached the disaster area, I knew I must break the law. Soon I spotted a welcome "No U-turn" sign. Now, I do not recommend illegal acts, but right then it was either make a break or inflict the preaching of a mentally unbalanced intern on the young parishioners of a church in Seattle. Hoping the nearest Illinois state patrol officer was grabbing a bite to eat somewhere in the floods downtown, I whipped around the concrete divider, and we kept on moving.

We eventually made it to the great Northwest, but not without further incident. Our tailpipe chose to separate from us in North Dakota, an earthshaking occurrence. My pregnant topside rider was somewhat taken aback at our car suddenly emulating the sound of a fighter jet. She still considers it fortunate that we did not require the services of a Fargo midwife.

The first night in our new apartment, I was overcome with acute separation anxiety. How I longed to be cradled by our Therapedic pillowtop mattress. Someday my dream would come true—when the moving van arrived.

Pulling my overcoat closer to my chin, I rearranged my body on the bedroom floor. Slowly I drifted into a troubled sleep, anesthetizing myself with the thought that at least our nightmarish journey had come to an end.

Frankly, I would be satisfied with just one more move in my lifetime. I could move to a land that is fairer than day where, I believe, a place awaits me that I'll never need or want to leave. "In my Father's house are many rooms; if it were not so I would have told you. I am going there to prepare a place for you. And . . . I will come back and take you to be with me that you also may be where I am" (John 14:2, 3).

I'm eager to make *that* move. How 'bout you?

Truth Tip #10

Choose Your Words Wisely

FAIR ENOUGH

If every witty comeback I never spoke could be harnessed for its cumulative kilowattage, the resulting power could light the Yukon Territory for the next decade.

I'm especially frustrated that the perfect poignant line always surfaces about twenty minutes too late. "I sure wish I'd thought of saying that" echoes down the hollowed halls of my mind almost daily.

You will be heartened to know, however, that I have developed a plan aimed at resolving this irritating issue. The secret to witty comebacks is advance planning. Stack a supply of penetrating sayings in storage, ready for quick retrieval at the critical moment, and listeners will reel in astonishment at your lightning-quick response-ability.

To help you learn, I have compiled a list of weighty maxims. These adages pack more punch than most because I have combined portions of two sayings to form one pithy couplet. These meet a wide range of conversational needs using a single utterance. Here are a few examples:

"The early bird gets . . . an island."

"No man is . . . a rolling stone." (The world of music contains a handful of exceptions to this.)

"A friend in need . . . gathers no moss."

"A bird in the hand . . . is worth a thousand words." And so forth.

A simple compilation like this provides a meaningful and impressive response for virtually any situation. If I had only known this at an earlier age, the Bubba's Ticket Booth incident might have gone something like this . . .

With the county fair in full swing, many a midsummer night's scream filled the air. In front of the Tilt-a-Whirl, Monkey

Barrels, Cosmic Blastoff, and even the traditional Ferris wheel, long lines of people waited.

This year, I had invited the Brawley brothers to join me at the festivities. Mom deposited us boys at the front gate, then backed around and spun off in the opposite direction. A little too happily, I thought.

Inside the fairgrounds, Lester spoke. "Whaddaya guys wanna do first?"

"I'd like to see the vegetable displays," I replied.

The brothers quickly squashed that idea. It seemed that Spike was more interested in the "Turbo Tank," a new ride that boasted it would "Turn Your World Upside Down and All Around." Envisioning a mighty gastric disaster, I declined the invitation to join the Brawleys in the Tank, though I vowed to support them from the sidelines.

As I stood and watched, I noticed an empty ticket booth standing near the bumper cars. Apparently, on this first day of the fair, the bashmobiles weren't up and running yet. A sly idea filled my cranial cavity. *I'm going to sneak into that ticket booth, then jump up and surprise Spike and Lester by pretending I'm the ticket man. It'll be funny!*

As luck would have it, the Brawley brothers' attention had drifted elsewhere, perhaps to the stellar performance of a Turbo Tank clean-up man. Sensing the right moment had come, I slipped through the rear door of the ticket booth. Inside, my heart leaped for joy as I spotted a *full roll of bumper car tickets waiting to be sold!* What more could I need to complete my act?

Suddenly, with the flair of a true circus showman, I stood to my full height, waved a raft of the ride passes, and began calling out, "Get your tickets here! Free tickets to the Bang-'em-Up Bumper Cars! Ha-ha!"

The Brawleys turned toward me. Something seemed to be keeping them from sharing in the humor of the moment. I became curious as their countenances took on a look that said something horrible was about to happen.

Disappointed, I turned to leave the ticket booth. That's when Bubba, as I shall call him, introduced himself.

Judging from his build, Bubba must have had both a Chicago Bears linebacker and Genghis Khan somewhere in his lineage. I discerned also that he had been singlehandedly supporting a major metropolitan tattoo shop.

Suddenly, I felt as though I were walking on air. A glance at my feet confirmed that this was indeed the case. As Bubba lifted me skyward by my shirtfront, I noted that the ride operator's well-tanned biceps resembled greased rocks. This would not bode well, I reasoned, for my physical self, should things take a turn for the uglier. Just then I remembered an important fact: We had Bubba outnumbered! Spike and Lester were with me!

"Look at those muscles!" Spike said, mouth agape.

"Like greased rocks!" Lester confirmed.

I knew that my physical self was in deep trouble.

Just then Bubba began gently inquiring as to my intentions, displaying the sensitivity training he received from the staff at Slick Louie's School of Communication and Jackhammer Services.

"What do you think you were doin' in that ticket booth?" he demanded, incorporating a broad selection of expletives.

I looked down at him from my lofty perch. "Well, I was just foolin'—"

"I'll tell you what you were doin' in there," Bubba went on, still holding me in suspense. "You were tryin' to steal bumper-car tickets, that's what you were tryin' to do, weren't ya?"

"No, you've got it all wrong . . ." My mind raced for a way out of this guilt-by-appearance situation. Then it hit me. Not Bubba's fist, but the solution to my problem. What I needed was a poignant witticism. If ever there were a critical moment, this was it! Surely a pithy phrase would disarm Bubba, hopefully before he dis-armed me.

My shoulders relaxed. Curving my lips into a confident smile, I locked eyes with my antagonist, which wasn't too hard since his eyes were now about half an inch from mine.

"Friend," I said with conviction, "blood is thicker than the mother of invention."

"Huh?" he said, drawing back.

I bore down on my tormentor. "One bad apple spoils the eye of the beholder."

He released his grip. "I never thought of it that way before."

I finished him off with a stunning double axiom. "You've got to stop and smell the gift horse in the mouth."

The man began to weep. I knew that I had broken him. "You're right!" he wailed. "I'm so sorry! Never again . . . never again." After exchanging addresses and phone numbers, we parted, knowing that this encounter had bonded us as bosom buddies forever.

Like I said, that's how it *could've* happened if I had known the value of sagacious verbiage. Unfortunately, the *real* closure to this incident involved Bubba bidding me adieu in more forceful terms.

"You listen and you listen good, you skinny little good-for-nothing runt of a ticket thief! Don't you let me see your face around here the rest of this fair, you hear me? Now move it!"

Sensing that our dialogue had drawn to a close, I shut my eyes and tried to enjoy my plummet to earth. Although it was a heady experience, I must say that a parachute would have been a welcome addition to my trendy fair-going attire.

I hereby affirm that another element must come into play before a pithy adage succeeds. You must say the *right thing* at the *right time*. In fact, that's not much different than the message of this Proverb from a *truly* wise guy: "A man finds joy in giving an *apt* reply, and how good is a *timely* word (Proverbs 15:23).

I couldn't have said it better myself.

Truth
Tip #11

Send
Your Pride
Packing

"PRIDE GOES BEFORE DESTRUCTION, A HAUGHTY SPIRIT BEFORE A FALL" (PROVERBS 16:18).

BONE OF CONTENTION

I spend the majority of my time in my right mind. That's the side of the brain responsible for such things as taking perfectly good words from the English language and turning them into books like this one. The other side of the brain, of course, is what's left.

I, even I, understood long ago that the chances of actually scratching out a living as a writer are somewhat lower than an earthworm's abdomen. No, I would prepare myself for a real job by getting a genuine education.

My report cards attest to the ups and downs of my academic life. History proved to be one of the more serious challenges to my receiving a diploma. At the historical *faux pas* recorded on quizzes bearing my name, the teacher must have wept. To this day I wonder who Augustus was and what crime the woman committed that demanded Augustus seize her. Many things from the past remain a mystery to me.

Yet for a brief period, something from "prehistory" managed to secure my deepest affections. It began the day they found The Bone.

My parents required the services of the Acme Septic Tank Company at one time. To delve into the reasons for this would only muddy the waters of the Bone story. Suffice it to say that we needed a new tank. Dad arranged for the groundbreaking ceremonies to begin at 7:00 one morning.

I looked forward to witnessing septic-tank installation first-hand. I had discovered that a well-told, exciting, first-person story did much to win friends and influence pals at school. Immersing myself in this development would add a colorful thread to my somewhat depleted skein of playground yarns.

Early next morning a roaring sound rocked our driveway. Pulling back the curtain, I peered out at a large red truck with a bulldozer riding piggyback on its flatbed trailer. Two burly men

66

in plaid flannel shirts and blue jeans sat inside. A gravelly voice said, "OK, let's see what we've got."

The men climbed out and headed around the house to the other side of the yard. I sped through the living room and found a prime viewing spot out the kitchen window, arriving just in time to catch the flip side of the action. I strained my ears, hoping to pick up some septic tanker terminology.

"This oughta be about the right place," one man surmised, pointing at the ground. Regardless of the mind-boggling technical jargon, I was determined to stick with it.

"Ernie," he continued, "why don't you bring the Caterpillar over here. I'll get the shovels."

"OK, Bud," Ernie agreed and headed off toward the truck and trailer.

I became concerned that the operation might require more time than I imagined. After all, one lonely little caterpillar could only hold out for so long. I breathed a sigh of relief as Ernie wheeled the huge yellow earthmover off the trailer.

By now, I had slunk out the back door and positioned myself behind a chestnut tree. Ernie began scooping out bucketfuls of earth and depositing them in a pile. Seldom had I enjoyed such before-school entertainment.

I was thinking Ernie had made good, deep progress when the steady rhythm of the bulldozer ceased. Swinging out of his cage, Ernie meandered over to the spot where he had been digging and gazed into the hole. Bud walked up to him.

"What are you starin' at?" Bud asked.

With a puzzled look, the brawny bucketer pointed to the wall of the shaft and said, "Right there, sticking out of the dirt. It looks like a big . . . *bone*." He dropped down into the hole and, with a quick jerk, pulled the object free. Tossing it over the brink, he climbed back out.

The men stood over their discovery. From my distant vantage point, I could see something that resembled a gigantic bone, about two feet long and nearly as thick as the business end of a Louisville Slugger. Realizing that I might be privy to a major-league paleontological discovery, I made my way closer. If there was any fame to claim via this uncovered treasure, I wanted a cut of the action.

Ernie offered a scientific explanation of what kind of animal this object might represent.

"I recollect my cousin Larry sayin' he saw somethin' like this in *National Geographic*. I think what we got here is a bone belongin' to one of them big, hairy prehistoric beasts. A 'Master Don,' I think Larry called it."

Under other circumstances, I might have doubted this hypothesis. But recently I had stumbled across a television series dealing with this particular period in prehistory. It would be a tough task for anyone to discredit such a well-researched program as *The Flintstones,* I thought.

Certain that I had the solid support of Bedrock behind me, I decided to let the news fly.

"Hey, Mom!" I yelled toward the house. "Come out here and see what *we* found! It's a Master Don bone!"

The men wheeled around and stared in my direction.

"Where'd *he* come from?" Bud asked.

I knew I had to make the bone my own right then. Stepping closer, I began to plead my case.

"Uh, I've been watching you dig that hole," I said awkwardly. "I see you found a pretty big bone. That would sure be quite a thing to show the kids at school, wouldn't it?" I hit them with the subtlety of an air horn in a soundproof booth. But it worked.

"Hmm, I s'pose it would be, at that," Ernie said. Reaching down, he picked up the bone and handed it to me. Thanks to this generous man, I now had in my possession a genuine relic from prehistory.

Lugging the artifact back to the house, I threw a paper bag over each end and walked out the door to catch the school bus.

As the bus pulled up slowly, a thought occurred to me. What if there was a rule against bringing Master Don bones on the school bus? After all, there was a rule against most everything else. Stepping inside, I glanced apprehensively at the "Bus Rules" sign above me.

Rule 1: No standing up allowed in the bus.

Rule 2: No chewing gum allowed in the bus.

Rule 3: No profanity allowed in the bus.

My eyes scrolled down the list. No mention of carrying Master Don bones. With a sigh of relief, I plopped my precious skeletal remain on the seat and settled in for the ride. I fell deep in thought, wondering how one might create a tidal wave of curiosity in the classroom regarding the brown sacks. I figured if I played my Old Maid cards right, I ought to be in a position to barter for almost anything I wanted. My chance soon came.

"What's in the bag?" It was Sheila Peyton, a high schooler no less!

"Oh, something," I said.

"So what is it?"

"What'll ya give me?"

Sheila scrunched up her face and paused. "I've got a stick of Dentyne gum."

"OK," I replied, taking the bribe price into my grubby little hands. After the show, Sheila was pretty sure I got the better end of the bargain. High schoolers have lost their sense of wonder.

But at my institution of lower learning, The Bone proved a smash hit. At show-and-tell time, baby birds and Barbie dolls could not stand up to The Bone. The episode accomplished more than a case of Hostess Twinkies could hope to achieve in evoking the admiration of my compatriots.

I might have received this flow of veneration indefinitely had Mom not decided to seek a second opinion on my prehistoric ticket to fame. She asked me to bring home The Bone the next day so that an expert at the paleontology department of our local university could look at it. Why she thought someone with a Ph.D. would know more about organic matter than a septic tanker, I could not fathom. But I had received my orders, and that evening I dutifully returned with The Bone.

The following afternoon I burst through the back door, eager for the truth about The Bone so I could get on with being popular. Mom looked up from the spot where she typically spent idyllic summer afternoons.

"How was school?" she asked as she stood at the sink, scrubbing dried strawberry jam off my Yogi Bear breakfast plate.

"All right," I said. Enough small talk. "So, Mom, did you take The Bone to college?" I wanted the professor's bony fide stamp of approval.

"Well, yes, I did," she replied with a conspicuous lack of enthusiasm.

"So what did he say?" I pressed. "Did The Bone come from a big, hairy beast?"

"Well, yes, it did . . ."

"I knew it was true!" I shouted, gyrating in celebration.

I have since learned that this is how members of the *Gulliblus maximus* species react just before they succumb to a sudden reality attack.

"The thing is," Mom continued, "the professor doesn't think The Bone came from a mastodon at all."

"Oh, really?" I replied, overlooking Mom's error in pronunciation and veering only slightly from my course of self-destruction. "Well then, what *did* The Bone once belong to?"

Painting a word picture of my post-reality-check ego would be in poor taste. Let's just say that my days of psuedo-admiration and free Dentyne gum were over. My story didn't have a leg to stand on, a condition it shared with the cow whose body part I now held. I had made a mammoth mistake.

As the dark cloud of truth enveloped me, I felt a sense of deep loss. Some of this arose from knowing that there would be no revenue rolling in from my proposed Six Flags Over the Septic Tank Theme Park and Master Don Museum. But mostly it was a loss of pride.

Later that week I packed The Bone away in the back of my bedroom closet. Maybe I'd think of something else to do with it someday, though I sensed that the uses of a dead cow's leg would be limited.

I close this bone-chilling tale with a charge: Ask God to "deep-six" (septic tanker lingo for "bury") any selfish pride in your life. Then make every attempt to prevent its resurrection. It's best to keep some things underground.

Dig?

Truth Tip #12

Know When to Change Course

SHIP OF FOOLS

It happens at least once in every male teenager's life—the call to pit one's self against the forces of nature. My call to nature seemed especially pitiful.

"So, do you think you can go camping with my family next weekend?" my friend Albert asked me over the phone. "We'll be taking our tent," he said, "and our canoe."

Neither tent camping nor canoeing had, thus far, played a major role in my life. I pictured myself stalking through the wild north woods. As the leader of the column, I hacked a trail for those portaging the canoe behind me. Spotting a pair of fiery eyes glaring at me from behind a clump of bushes, I froze in my tracks. Was it a mountain lion, or possibly a grizzly? I knew that I could not kill; as a natural man, I had pledged to protect life, not take part in its destruction. At that moment, I determined that no death would befall the forest this day—especially not mine. Switching my imagination into fast forward, in the next two and a half seconds I cleared a 35 mile path, scaled Mt. Hood, and rocketed down the Snake River.

"That sounds pretty good," I replied as calmly as I could, slightly out of breath and wiping perspiration from my forehead. "Where are we going?"

"The Wisconsin Dells!" he said with commendable spirit. In my mind I questioned his parents' choice of rugged country and challenging waterway. From an earlier vacation with my family, I knew that this Midwestern tourist mecca sat by a river that flowed with all the fury of molten lava. The only whitewater in the region hailed from the drain line connected to the automatic dishwasher at the Hiawatha Inn. Eventually, though, I came to understand the wisdom of their selection.

Campsites in civilized recreation areas sport certain amenities nearby. I flushed with embarrassment at having overlooked this truth.

The following Friday we left southwestern Michigan and began our north-by-northwest trek up Interstate 94. The drive itself proved breathtaking, largely because of the air quality around scentual Gary, Indiana.

After a few hours and 200 "See Tommy Bartlett's Water Show" billboards, we arrived at our destination, deep in the heart of cheese country. Albert's parents found a campsite, and we began pitching our respective tents, something I later regretted not doing in the broader sense of the word and opting for the feather beds at the Hiawatha Inn. While Albert's folks would be sheltered in the time of storm inside the "family" tent, Albert and I would bask in the expansive luxury of the "pup" version, a name apparently derived from the fact that it is slightly smaller than the average doghouse.

Our camp finally laid out, we dug into a hearty supper of Grape Nuts cereal and other woodsy grub. Darkness began to close in. As the wick on the Coleman lantern waned, we doused the fire and coughed our way to a fitful night's sleep in Badgerland.

By the time morning broke, I had formed the belief that the terra firma mattress had broken my back. The pain reassured me that I had not quite reached a state of total spinelessness. As I debated whether or not to call in dead, my tent-mate reached over and shook me, suggesting it was time to rise up to our aquatic adventures. Less than persuaded, yet not wanting to dampen my friend's enthusiasm, I roused my aching body. We downed a breakfast of campfire cakes and Grape Nuts, then said farewell to Albert's parents. With canoe in tow, we made our way to the banks of the nearby Wisconsin River.

We launched the craft into the water, and Albert tossed the paddles and life jackets into the bottom of the boat, along with a roll of convenience paper. With an air of authority he said,

"You can sit up front. I'll shove us off and then jump in."

I resented his suggestion immediately. If I were in front, I could not sit in the back. Although hardly a professional paddler, I had learned a few things about the various responsibilities incumbent on the two positions. While the front person provided a great deal of the vessel's propulsion, the rear admiral decided just how to employ such. Sudden moves to the right or left, or turning completely around, could be executed at will from the back seat. And emergency maneuvers such as avoiding rocks and rapids and Tommy Bartlett's employees were all controlled from the hindquarters, without consultation of the front crew member.

Discomforted by the situation, I had to choose one of two alternatives. I could remain silent and humbly submit to the current proposal, or I could stand up and voice my objection. After pondering the possible ramifications of rebelling, I accepted the expediency of not making waves, lest I be seen going overboard, with Albert's assistance. Harboring no grudge (at least not on the surface), I climbed aboard and settled in. Surely my trusted friend would steer me right.

Albert eased the canoe farther out into the water. Upon reaching knee-deepness, he hopped into the hull and delicately made his way to the rear seat. From this enviable position he would guide us full-steam ahead to a near-disaster at sea.

Our first half-hour out proved relaxing. We soaked up the early-morning peacefulness of the river. Thus far I had not been forced to overexert myself, and my friend had done an admirable job of navigating. Things were flowing smoothly. This might have continued, had the Wisconsin Dells Boat Tour paddle boat stayed at its mooring. Instead, it proceeded on its first run of the day.

I spotted "The Queen of the Dells" about 100 yards off port side. Albert's gaze remained fixed off starboard.

A mere 30 minutes earlier, though disgruntled, I had purposed in my heart not to become a "front seat driver." I now found myself toying with the idea of breaking this vow. A quick calculation suggested to me that, though the Wisconsin River resembles the Indian Ocean width-wise along that section, the two boats would shortly become one unless my companion changed course.

While a voice inside me shouted, "Say something, oh idiot, before thou descendest to a watery grave!" another voice whispered, "O ye of little faith. Dost thou not trust thy bosom buddy to take heed of the danger set before thee?" Deciding to invest complete confidence in Albert, I bolstered my waning courage and placed my tongue on hold.

As the gap shrank to 20 yards, I found it difficult to hold my resolve. My pal's commitment to survival at sea was in serious doubt. Thankfully, just as I was gathering sufficient oxygen for a blood-curdling scream, my one-man steering committee turned and caught a glimpse of the Queen. Apparently we would avoid a royal mess after all.

Appearances can be deceiving, however. After acknowledging the presence of her highness, Albert continued on his course. In a last-ditch effort to rationalize my psychotic seatmate's actions, I wondered if he might not be issuing a challenge of some sort. But I had little interest in discovering just who was the biggest chicken of the sea at this point.

The time had come to intervene, and I engaged my mouth in the panic position. But I had waited too long. The air I might have employed was suddenly usurped by the mighty blast of a horn. Then I heard the cutting of the boat's engines and watched as a small crowd of passengers gathered on the deck nearest our craft.

At this, even Albert sensed the error of his way. As if to confirm his injudiciousness, the Queen's jolly skipper made his way to the front of the group and launched into a salty discourse on seafaring etiquette. I am confident this recitation never earned the Good Housekeeping Seal of Tactfulness.

After the commander's speech and the accompanying wave of derision had subsided, Albert and I discovered previously unimagined reserves of energy. Pooling our collective humiliation, we revved up to around 135 ppm (paddles per minute) and sped off in the opposite direction. At least we had missed a collision.

At an opportune time later that hour, I queried Albert about his (in)actions.

"Say, Albert," I asked nonchalantly, trying to vent in an appropriate manner. "I was wondering why you nearly killed us both a short while ago."

He looked up at me as if amazed at my ignorance of nautical protocol.

"It's my rule that the smallest boat always has the right of way," he explained. "And that captain could see easy enough that we were just a little dinghy."

"I'm sure he noticed," I replied.

After our wild river ride, I concluded that one should heed two commandments about camping/canoeing trips. First, be willing to head in a new direction when the circumstances suggest it, if you get my drift. The second rule is a little more specific. Don't go canoeing with Albert. You might end up in the same boat.

Truth Tip #13

Grow Strong in Jesus

"He said to me, 'My grace is sufficient for you, for my power is made perfect in weakness.' Therefore I will boast all the more gladly about my weaknesses, so that Christ's power may rest on me" (2 Corinthians 12:9).

Elm Chip Surprises

My brother and I got an early start in the gourmet-food business. At the time, our establishment was less than 10 years old, as were its proprietors. Nevertheless, we had hit on an hors d'oeuvre we believed was guaranteed to succeed. We dubbed these treats Elm Chip Surprises.

It was not difficult to make an Elm Chip Surprise. No baking involved, and no messy cleanup. Best of all, during some seasons of the year we had access to a free, unlimited supply of our secret ingredient.

We prepared one of these little delicacies by plucking a leaf from one of the elm trees in our yard and placing it between two potato chips. *Voila*, an Elm Chip Surprise! Simple, but savory. Adding extra ingredients would detract from its one-of-a-kind flavor. We knew of nothing like it on the market, and the competition could only wish they'd thought of it first. With no overhead and plenty of opportunity for branching out, we figured the sky was the limit.

Our mother figured differently. Upon discovering her sons' green cuisine, she became certain that she had two clients for the Poison Control Center. Shortly thereafter, the doors to Dave 'n' Randy's Chip Yard closed forever. I admit that even I became a bit queasy a few years later when I learned that Dutch elm disease had claimed the lives of those very trees.

Mom informed us that some things in life just don't belong together; that certain combinations could even make people sick. At first I thought she was talking about my brother and me. It took me a while to realize she meant the Elm Chip Surprises.

Mother was probably right about what we thought was fine food. But my brother and I may have surrendered our enterprising aspirations too quickly, just because the Elm Chips were down. I have discovered since then that some things in life *do* go together that logically should not.

I call examples of this phenomenon—in which two opposites actually combine to form a like—"oppalikes." Oppalikes do not reside merely in the twisted minds of elementary-school entrepreneurs. The rational, adult world furnishes us with an abundance of such oddities.

Take, for example, bittersweet chocolate. Here we have a blatant oppalike. Not only does it *sound* terrible, but it is an impossibility. If the chocolate is bitter, how can it be sweet? If the stuff is sweet, how can it be bitter? Absurd. But Milton Hershey made many a dollar from such "non"-sense.

Etymologists have their own term for oppalikes. *Oxymorons* are words that shouldn't go together but do. "Reginald was sadly amused" represents a fine specimen of an oxymoron, or literary oppalike. Some writers carry this to extremes. James Thurber once used the term "a little bit big." That seems a little bit ridiculous to me. Any good writer should know better than that. I do. But then, you'll find James Thurber's name in the dictionary, but not mine. Maybe I'm just a little bit big for my britches.

Perhaps you've driven through a community of young, upwardly mobile professionals. If so, you've probably seen this oppalike: the run-walk. *How can this be?* I ask myself. Logically, a person could do one or the other, but not both at the same time. And if you have ever seen a run-walker in full swing, you'll agree with me that you wouldn't be caught dead doing something like that. But a doctor might say that you could be caught dead if you *don't* do something like that. As odd as it may appear, the run-walk seems to have its place.

Believe it or not, the Bible harbors an occasional oppalike. One of the all-time greats is the *weak strong man* of 2 Corinthians 12:10. Here, Paul uses true oppaliktic form:

"That is why, for Christ's sake, I delight in weakness, in insults, in hardships, in persecutions, in difficulties. For when I am weak, then I am strong."

On the whole, only politicians can get away with such double-talk. But if you look closely, Paul's statement actually makes a great deal of sense. The apostle knew that when his self-will was weakest, divine power could make him strongest.

With that, I must begin to end. I hope these few thoughts haven't left you clearly confused. If they have, drop by sometime, and we'll discuss it over lunch. Just be sure to call first. I can find the potato chips nearby, but the nearest elm tree is miles away.

Truth
Tip #14

Get the
Other Side
of the Story

LEAN ON ME

Johnny: I once had a very skinny friend.
   Audience: How skinny was he?
   Johnny: He was so skinny, he got hauled into traffic court for impersonating a parking meter.

King Eglon would likely not have found himself the victim of a parking meter mix-up. The Bible says, "Now Eglon was a very fat man" (Judges 3:17, RSV). Kind of a big shot in the broadest sense of the term.

While this mean-spirited monarch treated the Israelites of old less than kindly, I must confess that I covet his fatty-tissue test results. For while Eglon qualified as a weighty figure, I am a credentialed skinny person. I closely resemble the "before" picture in the Charles Atlas body-building course. "After" status continues to elude me. I had almost no girth at birth, and to this day remain in a state of semi-weightlessness.

Not that being of slender persuasion is a problem in and of itself. Rather, the world at large proves insensitive to the plight of the terminally slight. In the hope that I can affirm the value of viewing life from another's perspective, allow me to illustrate.

A large customer entered the furniture store where I worked as a college student. Being an unbiased salesperson, I strode quickly over and welcomed him to our establishment.

"Hello there!" I greeted. "How can I help you today?"

"I'm looking for a mattress," he replied matter-of-factly. Then, without breaking his stride, he added, "You sure are skinny. Have you been sick?"

Now wait a minute. What had I done to deserve this abuse? Perhaps I should rebut with something like "Welcome to our store, huge person. Have you been hitting the chocolate eclairs again?" Realizing that instigating a battle over his bulge (which was no small thing) would amount to the very model of bad witnessing, I held my tongue and directed him to the king-size beds.

Perhaps it's resentment that elicits certain disparaging remarks. Some people must think that the thin person purposely chooses a life of skinniness. That way, they can be a constant source of chastisement to their fleshy friends. But these same individuals must be made to realize that the naturally thin person's weight is usually beyond his or her control. Nothing within their power can change the fact that they wear a flat tire where many carry a spare.

Aesthetically speaking, thin is very in for both men and women. Recognize, however, that you can distinguish between stylish and unstylish thinness. The determinants are the amount of time, energy, and money expended to achieve one's emaciated appearance. Did you attain your sleek figure by spending countless hours at the local health spa? Or have you looked like a walking skeleton since the womb? More than one thin person has plummeted headlong off the ladder of social success with the wrong response to that question.

Food producers provide little help for the singular needs of the slender spender. The next time you're in the grocery store, take a good look around. You've arrived in a virtual land of paradise for the dedicated *dieter*. In the freezer case, *Lean Cuisine* abounds, while over in aisle 3-B, rivers of low-cal dressing flow freely. Obviously, with offerings like these, it is possible for any determined weight-loser to score a mighty victory.

But can a person find similar foodstuffs designed with the *underweight* in mind? Fat chance. Have you ever seen a box of "Big Daddy's Food for Skinny People" on the shelf? When did you last spy a staple product touted as "Blubber Bread—Helps Build Portly Bodies 7 Different Ways"? Oh, but what about those "high-protein food supplements," you say. If you have ever tasted one of these laboratory accidents, you have already counted out that option.

Some will undoubtedly claim that a steady intake of icecream and candy bars will accomplish the task. But ingesting several pounds of sugar each day exceeds the recommended daily allowance of sweet bliss, as set forth by such health-minded groups as the National Organization for the Termination of Pleasure in Eating (NOTPIE). Besides, what value are "empty" calories to those who need the full-bodied, genuine article?

On the brighter side, I have discovered some situations that place those who share my trim physique in a somewhat enviable position.

For example, I can change the oil on most cars without a grease pit. The procedure resembles the way a student slides a late paper under a teacher's door. Me being the paper, of course.

The thin person excels at locating a vacant spot in any "standing room only" event. Why? Not only do we have no spare tire, but for many of us, our rear bumpers are missing also.

The slender person enjoys a clear advantage during time of war. By simply turning sideways, the thin soldier stands a much greater chance of dodging the bullet on any given battlefield than does his or her more corpulent counterpart. In addition, should fighting develop in rural areas, the capacity to instantly camouflage oneself as a fencepost carries significant benefit.

Having weighed the evidence, it is obvious that the thin person has little, if nothing, of which to be ashamed. We have only begun to discover our full potential. So, on behalf of all my skinny compatriots, I urge humanity to walk a mile in the other person's shoe (no matter what size it might be) before passing judgment.

In the meantime, my fellow metabolical misfits, be of good courage. We must gird up our lanky loins and hold our single chins high. It is worth every ounce of effort we can muster if even one thin person can grow from our example. I make no bones about it—we face a great challenge. We lift our corporate burden as we rally around the battle cry of those who have gone before us:

"What have we got to lose?"

Truth Tip #15

Learn to Discern

BAT IDEA

Pow! Wham! Kazowie! The hero of Gotham City was about to
send another crook home with a headache.

Mom and Dad didn't care for *Batman*—too much violence.
They were right. Batman's preference for flattening faces was
hardly a Christian approach to problem-solving.

Sometime before my parents' *Batman* ban came into effect, I
caught a couple snatches of the show. The left hooks and upper-
cuts didn't appeal to me, but the Bat*cave* grabbed my interest. Not
only packed with the latest secret-agent electronic stuff, it had a
remote-controlled door that the crime-fighter's car both blew out
of and flew back into after its midnight crime-fighting missions.
Who could resist a cave's hidden entrance built right into the side
of a hill?

Boy, would I love to have something like that at home! I pictured myself leaping into my sleek, high-powered wheels—in
my case, Mom and Dad's 1968 Plymouth station wagon. *With a
flick of my skinny wrist the vehicle's engine roared to life, and I pressed
the button to raise the hidden door. Flooring the accelerator, I sped out
of the cave and onto U.S. Highway 31. Soon I returned, another heroic
crime-stopping mission behind me.* The only element missing—besides a driver's license—was Batman's sidekick, Robin. But I
knew it was a birdbrained idea to think that I could support him
on *my* allowance.

I sighed longingly. If only I had a car cave of my own . . .

"I guess they sell electric garage door openers at Sears," my
pal Tomahawk Stiles ventured at school the next day. "Why do
you want to know?"

"Oh, I'm just thinkin' about building something," I replied
casually. If Tomahawk knew I was toying with the idea of carv-

ing out a Batcave in the side of my parents' property, he'd fall victim to ULS—uncontrollable laughter syndrome. I was thinking of his health.

Tomahawk pressed me. "Maybe I can help you build it, whatever it is. I can't help you buy a garage door opener, though. I don't have any money."

I knew the chances of Tomahawk having any cash were about as likely as Mom filling her bedroom bookshelves with Batman comics. But one thing my pal did have—muscles. Big muscles. The kind that, put to a shovel, could turn more earth than a battalion of hyperactive moles. But he could help only if he didn't laugh himself to death first.

"I'll let you know when I've got a few more details worked out," I said.

"Whatever. Hey, do you want to come over tonight and watch TV?"

"Not tonight. I've got plans."

"Oh."

That evening I sauntered past the garden and down the hillside of our property. I made sure Mom and Dad and my brother, Dave, hadn't noticed my exit since I was concerned for their health too.

The cave concept required some essentials. First, in the spirit of secrecy, I would have to install a tunnel from our basement to the cave, maybe six feet high and three feet wide. Second, the cave itself would have to be large enough to house our station wagon, which was about as long as the country of Chile. I would need a crossbeam strong enough to support a garage door, as well as an occasional roof support in the tunnel. All this would help me avoid having a tombstone bearing these words:

> "Of R. S. Fishell
> There ain't no more;
> If only he'd gone
> To the lumber store"

I surveyed the slant of the hill and the distance to our house. Next I mentally measured the width and depth of cave space the station wagon would require. I calculated the amount of time it would take to earn enough money to purchase a garage door, an electric opener, and support beams, then whip them all into a Batcave. The projected time I came up with: about 85 years. Having Tomahawk on the job site could cut off a decade or so. But sooner or later he'd have to take time off—to eat, sleep, get married, and play with his grandchildren.

A thought hit me: I would be taking a huge risk. I'd heard that weird things happen to adult males—something about a "midlife crisis." What if, years later, I drove home after a hard day at the office, pulled into my half-finished cave, and began to think the whole idea was silly? Shaken at the thought, I trudged back up to the house.

"Saw ya over the hill," Dave commented as I reached the yard. "What were ya doin'?"

"Giving up," I said and strolled past him into the house. I figured some things were worth going for and some things weren't. In this case, it wasn't.

I never did tell Tomahawk about my proposed hole in the hill. He would have guffawed himself into convulsions and then called the closest mental health clinic and asked them to leave the light on for me. I guess the whole idea *was* a little crazy, but at least I'd had a chance to choose the best use of my time. Call it discernment. Which sometimes means calling it quits.

Truth
Tip #16

Use the
Library

HEART ATTACK IN THE STACKS

It started out like any other evening at the college library. Nothing unusual about it except that I was there in the library myself. I had not formed the habit of spending time expanding my mind. As a college student, I didn't want to ruin my days by letting classwork interfere. But a hefty term paper can bring out the scholar in even the poorest of pupils.

As I wandered the stacks trying to find suitable material on my topic (probably "The Upper Nubian Beetle Crisis of 1949") I happened to glance toward a study table. My heart skipped a beat. *Did I see what I thought I saw?* I had to check it out.

Making my way discreetly past the books about mosquito larvae, I halted near the termite section. Peering around the end of the row, I cast my eyes on the most attractive female creature this side of Upper Nubia. I immediately identified with the fifteenth section of the first movement of Solomon's song: "How beautiful you are, my darling!" With any luck she would soon be singing the next line, "How handsome you are, my lover! Oh, how charming!"

As fate would have it, the chosen one sat studying with another girl I knew casually. Here lay the perfect opportunity to renew an old friendship and begin a new one. I made my approach.

"Well, hello there, Londa! Long time no see!" My opener came out with all the originality of a peanut-butter-and-jelly sandwich.

"Oh, hi," she replied.

Despite the staggering creativity of the conversation, Londa's friend displayed her appreciation with a show of unbroken concentration. She didn't even move her head. I would have to think fast, lest my plans go irreversibly awry.

"Londa," I said, leaning a bit closer, "could I see you for a moment over in the bug section?"

Her friend finally raised a suspicious eyebrow. Londa, however, slid her chair out with a polite air and followed me to the back of the stacks. We stopped between fleas and grasshoppers.

"I'm going to get right to the point," I blurted. "I want the facts on the girl who's studying with you. Let's begin with her name. We can get more specific from there." I wanted critical information such as How big is her current boyfriend? A lack of tact on my part, perhaps, but it got the job done. I left the library with just the information I needed.

The rest, as they say, is history. Londa's friend, Diana, and I married in 1979. Now, some 45 years after the now-famous, albeit fictitious, Upper Nubian Beetle Crisis, the beetles may be dead, but the love bug is here to stay.

Let me leave you with a bit of wisdom from a formerly imprudent student: It pays to use the library. After all, I might still be single if I hadn't checked things out.

Truth
Tip #17

Prepare
to Succeed

"ONE WHO IS SLACK IN HIS WORK IS BROTHER
TO ONE WHO DESTROYS" (PROVERBS 18:9).

No Laughing Matter

Jon and I had earned a reputation as the class comedians. The
other kids constantly laughed at us. Now that I think about it,
this happened even when we weren't trying to be funny. For
whatever reasons, the junior-high talent night committee asked
Jon and I to host their annual show. What a break this could turn
out to be! Always happy to grab the spotlight, we accepted the
committee's offer.

As the official eighth-grade laugh staff, the responsibility for
our big gig weighed heavily on our underdeveloped shoulders.
Jon and I believed that any joke worth doing was worth doing
well. So, we decided, the most important thing would be to *dress*
like real comedians.

We had already heard on occasion that we looked pretty
funny. But Jon and I knew what would give us that professional
edge: turtleneck sweaters. At the time, this was a *very* groovy look.

We located two of these hip garments at JC Penney in South
Bend. Were we going to be cool, or what? In fact, those turtle-
necks would make us so cool that we wouldn't need to rehearse
our jokes. We'd just wing it, relying heavily on our coolness to
carry us through.

The big night upon us, Jon and I donned our turtleneck
sweaters and blazers, then headed on-stage to announce the first
act. We had decided to save our best stuff (which, frankly, was
worse than awful) for the moments when the judges declared
their decisions.

On and off the stage we ran, introducing the acts. Susie
Chan's 13-year-old fingers flew across the piano keyboard (fortunately she was able to retrieve them) as she pounded out "The
Flight of the Bumblebee." Stanley Roberts's South African accent
scored big points with the judges as he pranced across the stage

singing an Afrikaner folk song. Luellen Fritz played an unforgettable violin solo, the name of which escapes me.

Finally the performances finished, and the judges exited to tally the votes. Jon and I had reached those critical moments.

"Jon," I said to my partner, "did you hear Mike Finster got a new trampoline for his birthday?"

"No kidding?"

"That's right. He's jumping up and down with excitement!"

But if Mike Finster was bouncing off the ceiling, the crowd was not.

Come on, folks, I silently begged, *let's laugh it up a little. Your funny bones can stand the strain.*

"Randy," Jon came back, "do you know who the laziest person in the world was?"

"No," I replied. "Who?"

"Dr. *Dolittle!*"

After a few more meager attempts, we realized the seriousness of our situation. Not even our cool clothing seemed to work with this crowd. The laugh-'n'-scream team showed signs of falling apart at the seams.

Reeling from the deafening silence, we half-ran offstage to seek out help.

"Does anyone back here know any good jokes?" I pleaded with some of the performers. Finally a kid told me one about the president of the United States, Fidel Castro, and the pope riding together in an airplane. It sounded funny enough, so we headed back onstage, hoping this zinger would save us from a case of terminal embarrassment.

But somehow the punch line came out all twisted around. I dashed offstage again. Grabbing the original joke-teller, I asked, "What did you say the pope said?" Back onstage I gave it a second shot. But the wording still sounded wrong.

By now I had noticed the crowd growing restless. Audience members began turning to one another for entertainment, since they'd heard none onstage. Kind of a do-it-yourself approach to comedy. Suddenly a man called out from the midst of the tumult: "Play the piano!" I recognized the voice as my father's.

My dad knew that I had a knack for tickling the ivories. But I had stored in my musical memory banks only a few easy-to-play

Top 40 tunes. It seemed too much to ask the crowd to endure such fare, coming on the heels of genuine talent. No, that would be the cowardly thing to do.

Instead, we left the stage. I mean, why bother the audience when they were having such a good time on their own?

I don't remember who won the talent show. And you probably think I learned never to do anything like that again, right? Well, you're right—and you're wrong.

It's true that I never again wanted to do anything as *poorly* as I did it that evening. But I *did* want to serve others, should I ever again get the remote chance to do something in public. And, believe it or not, I did get the chance—many times.

How did I overcome the potentially devastating effects of that laughless evening? I learned to prepare so that I might reap the best results. I guess Jon must have slain the dragon of that depressing evening too. He's "onstage" every day as he teaches his medieval literature classes at the University of Arkansas.

By the way, did you hear about the telephone operator who pretended to be a talent show host? She wasn't too successful—the audience thought her jokes were phoney.

Truth
Tip #18

Let God
Lead You Where
He Needs You

"IN HIS HEART A MAN PLANS HIS COURSE, BUT THE LORD DETERMINES HIS STEPS" (PROVERBS 16:9).

MAJOR PROBLEMS

I spent four years as a college freshman. Not because of my IQ, but because I remained decidedly undecided.

My problems began on the first registration day. Having received a list of majors to choose from, I saw nothing that interested me. My adviser tried to help by suggesting I take "general" classes.

"You'll need the general credits regardless of your major," he said. As a conscientious objector, I wasn't interested in learning how to become a general. Later I discovered that I could take general classes without seeing combat duty.

Still another dilemma awaited me in the ID picture line. The photographer's assistant handed me a personal information card to fill out.

At the onset, it didn't look threatening. "Name." I knew that. "Address." So far so good. "Birth date." Cruising now. "Major." Foiled again.

I began to think, *Maybe I should just write "general" in the blank.* But no, if anyone saw "major general" under my picture, they'd think I was an army man for sure.

I looked over the list of options again. Biology, music, physics. On and on the list went, but nothing seemed to fit. I asked the photographer's assistant for help.

"Do you mean your major isn't *anywhere* on the list?" she asked.

"Well, you see," I replied, humiliated, "I haven't decided on a major yet. Isn't there some kind of all-purpose degree?"

With a disapproving look, she pointed to the blank on my card and said, "Why don't you just put down 'Undecided'?"

What other choice did I have? Officially I was just a class-hopper in the field of academics.

My second year as a freshman took a different course. I had decided on a major: social work. Helping others always made me feel good, so what could be better? Before long, however, I learned a cold, hard fact. A job as a social worker would require a master's degree. That would require much study. That thought soon required that I change majors. After all, I couldn't let social work interfere with my social life.

By the time my third freshman year rolled around, people had begun to drop hints.

"Your dad's CPA firm sure is going great guns," one person pointed out. "It won't be long before he'll need a junior partner."

Hmmm. Why not? I signed up for Accounting 101. But a slight problem arose. I couldn't figure out how the debits and credits functioned in those little columns. Balancing books made me dizzy.

Only in my fourth year as a freshman did I admit the truth: I needed professional help. Then an idea struck me. Why not become a psychology major? Maybe I could psychoanalyze myself and figure out why I was having so many major problems.

But that didn't last. Instead, for some reason—heaven only knows why—I chose theology and stuck with it. The best news is, I've never regretted it. It seems that Someone knew all along what would make me happiest and when I'd be ready to commit myself wholeheartedly to earning a sheepskin.

Maybe *you've* made it to the majors, but don't know what field to play. Or perhaps you're fed up with your current career but don't know what to do next. Either way, take heart. I've learned that if you stay in touch with God, He'll take you where He wants you to go, one degree at a time.

Truth
Tip #19

Keep Your
Thank Tank Full

HAVE YOU HUGGED YOUR VACUUM CLEANER TODAY?

As a child, I habitually crawled into bed with my bedroom light on. My parents might suddenly need me in the middle of the night, and I would always be ready.

This presented a problem. Eventually I would want to turn off my light, but I would have to leave a toasty warm bed. One night the idea for the "O'Fishell Lamp-O-Matic" came to me.

I attached a string to the switch on my wall-mounted bedroom light and wrapped the other end around my bedpost. Then, just before I drifted off to sleep, I would give the string a quick jerk. Sometimes it worked; other times I nearly pulled the light fixture off the wall. No matter—my career as an inventor had begun.

I've accumulated a respectable collection of practical inventions. Take the "Slop-Stopper" toothbrush. This toothbrush comes with a plastic sleeve that fastens around your wrist. The device prevents wet, foamy toothpaste and drool from running down your arm while you brush.

Then there's the "Humane Maze Mouse Trap." This gadget operates on the principle that any mouse will eventually keel over if driven to exhaustion. The Humane Maze trap, baited with mouse goodies, draws our fuzzy friends into an endlessly complicated system of miniature hallways. The mice become confused and eventually collapse, winded from their escape attempts. The happy homeowner then takes the still-unconscious little fellow or gal and releases her/him back into the great outdoors. Since mice think their natural habitat is your house, this invention finds constant use.

I must confess, people haven't exactly been beating a path to my door. The "Slop-Stopper" hasn't become a household word, and not a single issue of the *Rodent Review* has featured the "Humane Maze Mouse Trap" as the product of the year. My inventions are way ahead of their time, it seems.

It's probably all for the best. Most neat inventions are taken for granted sooner or later anyway. In fact, I've noticed several modern conveniences that have come to prominence since I was a kid which I already take for granted. For example:

The blow dryer

Now I will admit that certain antiquated hair-drying devices have been around for years. I've seen them at garage sales. But not until the early 1970s would a male even dream of being caught with one in his room. Now, several decades later, no one gives them a thought.

Before I owned a blow dryer I had to comb one side of my wet hair to the center of my head. I'd kneel over the living-room heat register until that section was baked dry. I would repeat the process on the other side to complete my "style." Of course, this was a seasonal hair procedure. Fortunately, with no school during the summer months, I could look like a ragtop and not care. I did face embarrassment at school one winter when my parents forgot to pay their fuel oil bill.

The fast-food franchise

Restauranteurs of bygone days were a ghoulish bunch. They took great pleasure in watching their customers starve to death. At least, that's how it seemed to a kid who was forced to wait half an hour for a strawberry shake.

Thanks to "fast food," we no longer wait. Now your meal is cooked *before* you order it. You don't even have to get out of your car. True, you now face a limited menu, and your cholesterol level soars to unparalleled heights shortly after you've partaken. For a nation that can't seem to slow down, fast food seems to meat the need.

The water bed

In the 1960s, only two types of creatures would risk sleeping on a mattress of water—ducks and hippies. We were content to let sleeping ducks lie then. As for the hippies, rumor had it that lying horizontally on H_2O could transform ordinary Z's into a mystical experience.

Today, water bed manufacturing has become a virtual science. Choose a "full-wave" or a "semi-wave" mattress, available in airy pastels or rugged earth tones. Back problems? Water beds are a dream come true for many a slipped-disc sleeper.

The compact disc

Many readers will recall a precursor to the CD known as the *record*. These "long playing" albums provided a helpful step toward in-home hi-fidelity entertainment, though they were not without their problems—without their problems—without their problems . . .

The *eight-track tape cartridge* was a sound development that allowed rhythm addicts to take their favorite tunes on the road. An added benefit was the character development that resulted from spending a romantic evening extracting the tape from the deck once it had accidentally wound itself around 47 different gears. Studies have shown that the *cassette tape* produces similar results in the area of personal growth.

Today the relatively trouble-free compact disc stands as a high-tech, tapeless tribute to the early efforts of audio pioneers. The strengthening of our moral fiber must be left to programming our VCRs.

The pressed wood log

Need a fire fast? This wood's for you. Never again will you waltz through the snow in your stockinged feet to find another log for the fire. Pick up a couple of these kerosene-coated sawdust wonders at the supermarket and store them in the pantry. Available in precise one-and-a-half- and three-hour sizes, your evening by the hearth stretches uninterrupted for as long as your log permits.

I felt guilty at first, not having earned the right to light up. Basking in the glow of an amber flame without first having to defrost my gangrenous toes seemed unethical. But the thought of saving my big pinkie from amputation has warmed me up to the idea.

The computer?

I place a question mark following this one because some of us don't take the computer for granted yet, although we're getting close. I do appreciate the fact that I am "processing" these words rather than employing that ancient instrument from my youth, the typewriter.

I suppose, as I already have the blow-dryer and the burger joints, I will one day take the computer for granted. So I strive to remind myself to, like the Levites of old, "stand every morning to thank and praise the Lord" (1 Chronicles 23:30) for amenities that carry some of life's burdens. After all, the inventors may make our life more pleasant, but it's the Creator who gives them the ability to make it happen.

That reminds me—I need to go finish a little more housework. So, thanks, Murray Spengler. At times like these, I appreciate that little invention of yours called the vacuum cleaner.

Truth
Tip #20

Just Say
Yes to Jesus

"For God so loved the world that he gave his one and only Son, that whoever believes in him shall not perish but have eternal life" (John 3:16).

No Cardboard Characters

I hope these foible-filled stories have brought you laughter and warmed your heart. Yet I would be a Christian unworthy of his calling (which I suppose we all are) if I left without asking you to give special thought to what I'm about to say.

The simple truths I've shared in this book are aimed at helping us become persons of greater character. But that can't happen if we're disconnected from Jesus Christ. It makes me think of those life-sized cardboard cutouts of famous people that vendors sell on street corners. They look real from a distance, but when you get closer, you see they're just flat fakes. Those "characters" blow over with the first stiff wind that comes along.

The secret to standing strong when storms of difficulty blow into your life is to anchor yourself in Jesus. If you haven't asked Him to forgive your sins and become your Saviour and Lord, then do it right now, through a simple prayer, and accept His long-standing invitation to a better life. Because there are already enough cardboard characters in this world. And they will all fall.